Lakes
of Victoria, BC

Adam Ungstad

Lakes
of Victoria, BC

Adam Ungstad

HIKE • WALK • SWIM • FISH • PADDLE • NATURE • HISTORY

To purchase larger quantities of this book at a discount, or to invite the author to speak at an event, please contact the publisher at the email address below. This book is also available in electronic and accessible formats.

www.secretlakes.ca · info@secretlakes.ca

ISBN 978-0-9880853-3-6

Front cover design and interior illustrations by Leechtown Design
Maps by Gillian Harvey and Mike Munroe
Editing by Eric Anderson
Design and layout by Common Foundry Design Studio
Printed in Canada by Friesens
Distributed in Canada by Heritage Group Distribution

MIX
Paper from
responsible sources
FSC® C016245

Front Cover Photograph: Paddling at Thetis Lake by Monty Wiseman
Back Cover Photograph: Sheilds Lake by Adam Ungstad

Disclaimer

Activities described in this book such as walking, hiking, swimming, fishing, boating, and paddling may all contain inherent dangers. Individuals must determine risk according to their abilities, use good judgement, and take responsibility for their actions.

The information in this book is true and complete to the best of the author's knowledge, but is not guaranteed to be completely accurate or reliable. Do not depend on any information in this book for your personal safety.

Different rules and regulations apply to the different places described in this book. It is the reader's responsibility to learn and comply with current regulations. Maps provided in this book are for general information purposes only, and should not be used for navigation purposes.

The author and publisher will not be liable for any damage, loss, or injury resulting from the use of information published in this book.

Contents

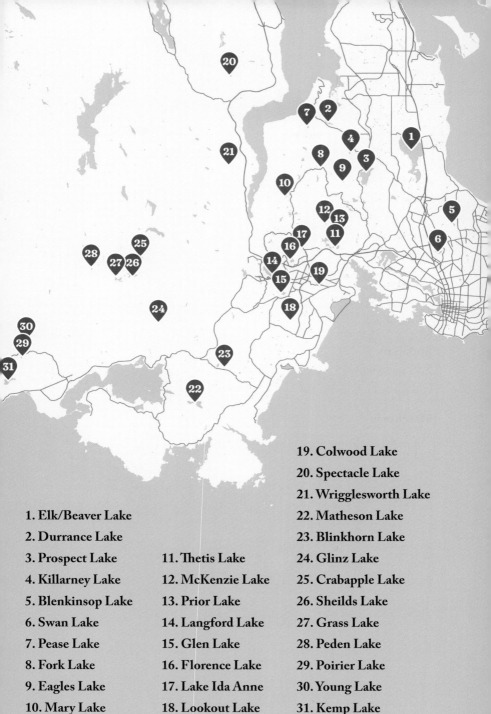

Quick Reference

Lake	Beach	Dock	Walking Trail	Hiking Trail	Fishing Pier
Blenkinsop Lake			✓		
Blinkhorn Lake			✓		
Colwood Lake					
Crabapple Lake				✓	
Durrance Lake	✓		✓	✓	✓
Eagles Lake					
Elk/Beaver Lake	✓		✓	✓	✓
Florence Lake			✓		✓
Fork Lake			✓	✓	
Glen Lake	✓	✓	✓		✓
Glinz Lake					
Grass Lake				✓	
Kemp Lake		✓			
Killarney Lake			✓	✓	
Lake Ida Anne					
Langford Lake	✓		✓		✓
Lookout Lake			✓		
Mary Lake			✓		
Matheson Lake	✓		✓	✓	
McKenzie Lake				✓	
Pease Lake				✓	
Peden Lake				✓	
Poirier Lake		✓	✓		✓
Prior Lake	✓	✓		✓	
Prospect Lake		✓	✓		
Sheilds Lake				✓	
Spectacle Lake	✓		✓	✓	
Swan Lake			✓		
Thetis Lake	✓		✓	✓	
Wrigglesworth Lake					
Young Lake					

Boardwalk	Boat Launch	Playground	Nature House	User-Friendly	Toilet
	✓			✓	✓
				✓	✓
	✓	✓	✓	✓	✓
✓				✓	
				✓	✓
✓	✓	✓		✓	✓
	✓			✓	✓
✓	✓	✓		✓	✓
					✓
			✓	✓	
					✓
	✓			✓	
	✓	✓		✓	✓
					✓
✓			✓	✓	✓
	✓			✓	✓

Introduction

There are hundreds of lakes on Vancouver Island. Some of them are in parks or nature sanctuaries, some of them are surrounded by houses, and many are out of sight, locked behind gates and at the end of logging roads.

Humans impact lake ecosystems, directly and indirectly. Even if you've never visited a lake, your actions still impact the life it sustains. Use this book to discover local watersheds, and get involved to protect all of Canada's freshwater lakes.

Acknowledgments

For Carly, Gabriel, and Georgia.

Thank you to my wife, children, family, and friends for supporting my work on this book over many years.

Thank you to everyone who has ever been a part of helping me explore this beautiful island. Sight loss makes access to nature a challenge, but you make it possible. I am grateful for your companionship.

Thank you to the many different governments, community associations, non-profit organizations, historians, academics, naturalists, advocates, and landowners who helped me make the best book possible. I am grateful for the knowledge you've shared and the work you do each day.

Thank you to other local authors and publishers who shared their knowledge of the book industry and continue to make inspiring books.

Thank you to the team responsible for the production and execution of this book, many of whom have been working with me on this project for over a decade.

Thank you for reading this book. I hope you enjoy it.

Adam Ungstad
Piers Island, BC
March 2021

How to use this book

This book gives quick access to practical information about Victoria's lakes and adds context of their nature and local history. You can use this book to find lakes for an activity you like, such as swimming, by reading the Activity lists.

The Lakes 101 section has answers to questions like who owns a lake, or what the major threats to lake ecosystems are. Each lake featured in this book has practical information on access, and maps are provided for all lakes with public access. Vignettes on local history, animals, and plants are interspersed throughout.

As you explore Victoria's lakes, be curious, observant, and respectful. Minimize your impact. Know and follow the seven principles of Leave No Trace. Learn more at: **www.leavenotrace.ca/principles**

About this book

This book is the successor to a book I wrote and self-published in 2012, called *Secret Lakes of Southern Vancouver Island*. The original book has been out of print for many years as I wanted to add more about the nature of lake ecosystems.

There are millions of lakes in Canada under threat of climate change, habitat loss, and invasive species. Lake ecosystems are interconnected through watersheds, and what happens hundreds of kilometers away can impact local lakes.

Lakes need people to protect them, and people will protect the things they know and love. This book was made to connect people with the local ecosystems they are a part of.

About the author

Adam Ungstad is a legally blind Canadian writer and naturalist with two passions: lakes and information architecture. He has been exploring and learning about Vancouver Island's lakes, nature, and local history for over 15 years.

Adam Ungstad has previously worked as a writer and editor for the World Health Organization, and currently splits his time between Vancouver Island and Geneva, Switzerland.

Indigenous territories and placenames

The lakes in this book lie within the territories of the Esquimalt and Songhees Nations, the Scia'new, T'Sou-ke, and Malahat First Nations, and the W̱SÁNEĆ (Saanich) Nations: BOḰEĆEN (Pauquachin), STÁUTW̱ (Tsawout), W̱JOȽEȽP (Tsartlip), and the W̱SE̱IKEM (Tseycum).

Indigenous peoples sustainably managed Vancouver Island's forests for hundreds of years before the arrival of colonial settlers, and have placenames for many landscape features. These placenames will be added in future editions of this book.

Many of the lakes in this book are thousands of years old. Indigenous history and stewardship practices must be applied to current land management practices to ensure these lakes continue to exist for thousands of years more.

PHOTO BY ADAM UNGSTAD

Lakes 101: All About Victoria's Lakes

What is a lake?

Beyond a basic definition such as "a large area of water surrounded by land" it becomes difficult to define what a lake is and isn't. The water's surface area, the water's volume, whether there are inflows or outflows (creeks), or whether light reaches the bottom are all different criteria used to define lakes. Another definition used by limnologists (people who study lakes) is if wind plays a major role in mixing the water.

Once you've chosen your favourite definition for what a lake is, you can start working on the differences between a lake, a pond, a slough, a loch, a lagoon, a reservoir, and a tarn!

What is a watershed?

The BC Lake Stewardship Society defines a watershed as,

> "The entire area of land that moves the water it receives to a common water body. The term watershed is misused if it describes only the land immediately surrounding a water body or the water body itself. The true definition represents a much larger land area than most people normally consider. A watershed is where much of the ongoing hydrological cycle takes place and it plays a crucial role in the purification of water."

A watershed is much more than just the shoreline around a lake or a river; watersheds include the hills, mountains, roads, lawns and even groundwater that all drain into a common place. Many watersheds on Vancouver Island are hundreds of square kilometers – close to Victoria, the Sooke River Watershed is over 340 km^2.

Smaller watersheds are often part of larger ones. For example, Peden Lake is the headwaters of the Mary Vine Creek Watershed. Yet, Mary Vine Creek flows into the Sooke River, making it also part of the larger Sooke River Watershed.

There are over 300 watersheds larger than 1 km² in the Capital Regional District, and thousands of smaller watersheds that are unnamed. A tiny, seasonal mountain stream can have a watershed as small as a few square meters.

How many lakes are there in Canada?

Natural Resources Canada estimates that there are around 31,700 lakes with a surface area over 3 km² in Canada. However, one of Victoria's largest lakes, Elk/Beaver Lake, has a surface area of less than 2 km², meaning it would not be included in that count.

Estimates vary, but it is generally accepted that there are 2 to 3 million lakes in Canada with a surface area under 3 km². If Canada's population is 38 million people, that leaves roughly one lake for every twelve people in the country.

How are lakes formed?

Many of Victoria's lakes, such as Langford Lake, are "kettle lakes", which were formed when glaciers melted over 10,000 years ago. Other natural processes that create lakes include erosion, dissolution, volcanoes, landslides, and even tectonic activity.

There are few, if any, lakes near Victoria that have not been modified by humans via dams that control outflows, culverts that redirect creeks, or other changes to water levels upstream. Eagles Lake in the highlands was created out of wetlands in the 1970s, and Elk/Beaver Lake was originally two different bodies of water.

Animals also create or alter lakes. For example, beavers deliberately make dams to influence water levels in a small lake or pond, which influences the entire surrounding ecosystem.

What makes a lake clear?

There are three natural factors that impact the clarity and colour of water in a lake: inorganic matter such as soil, organic matter such as decayed leaves, and algae such as phytoplankton.

Unnatural factors such as pollution or runoff can bring excess nutrients, which can also impact the clarity and colour of water in a lake, particularly in the case of algae blooms.

Lakes also change colour depending on viewing angle, the time of day, and the weather.

The clarity of water in a lake can be measured with a simple tool called a Secchi disc – a black and white disk that is lowered into water until it can no longer be seen, thereby showing the depth of light penetration.

What does it mean for a lake to "turn over"?

If you've ever been swimming in a lake you probably noticed that the deeper water gets, the cooler it is. Most lakes form layers (stratify), with the coldest water at the bottom.

Cold water is denser and resists mixing with water warmed by the sun near the surface during the summer. As the seasons change, water at the surface cools, which causes the water to mix and "turn over."

If the surface of a lake freezes over winter, the water at the bottom is then warmer than the ice at the top, meaning the lake will turn over again when the ice melts. Lakes that turn over twice a year are called dimictic lakes.

Most lakes in the Victoria area do not freeze over in the winter, meaning that they turn over only once a year, from November to April. These are known as monomictic lakes.

Can you drink from a lake?

Drinking from lakes and streams can be dangerous and is not advised. Feces from waterfowl and pollution from other sources can contaminate water with *Giardia* or *E. coli*. If you do not have your own water and need to drink, use a proper water filter or a fast-moving stream.

Cooling off at Peden Lake on a summer's day after the hike to get there.
PHOTO BY ADAM UNGSTAD

What makes a lake warm?

Elevation, sunlight, depth, and circulation each contribute to the temperature of water in a lake. Within a day trip from Victoria, elevation is a key factor. Spectacle Lake, with an elevation of 379 m, will generally be cooler than Thetis Lake, with an elevation of 59 m.

If you want a warm place to swim, look for a beach on the north or east shore of a lake, as these will get the most afternoon sun.

How long does water stay in a lake?

The amount of time it takes water to pass through a lake, or the pace at which water in the lake is replaced, is one of many factors that can affect the quality of water in a lake. A shorter retention time (or higher flushing rate) means that water moves from the lake's inflows to its outflows at a quicker pace. The replacement speed depends on many things, including the size of a lake and amount of precipitation.

For local context, a report produced by the BC Lake Stewardship Society indicates that Prospect Lake had a retention time of 0.8 years in 2012. The estimate for Elk Lake is 5-9 years depending on how it is calculated.

How do shorelines affect lakes?

Shorelines are key transition areas between water and land, and they provide some of the most valuable habitat of all terrestrial ecosystems. Shorelines are also popular places for humans.

Natural shorelines are riparian zones left to grow and develop as nature dictates, allowing for complex interactions between water, soil, microorganisms, insects, plants, and animals. They help prevent erosion and algae blooms because their vegetation filters out runoff from the surrounding land, keeping sediments, nutrients, and other pollutants out of a lake.

Altered shorelines have docks, retaining walls, or human-made beaches. They often suit the desires of people but overlook their impact on the surrounding lake ecosystem.

Some of Victoria's lakes have a portion of their shoreline bordering a park, and a portion bordering private land – such as McKenzie Lake or Fork Lake. It is difficult to access the water at these lakes as there are no docks or beaches. This lack of development is likely purposeful, done to ensure quality of life for residents and that a portion of the shoreline remains natural.

What are aquatic plants?

Aquatic plants are essential to healthy lakes. They provide shelter and habitat for young fish and insects, and they feed waterfowl and mammals. They hold sediment on the bottom and generate oxygen for all creatures to survive.

The type of aquatic plants in a lake depends on the nutrients in the water, the water's temperature and clarity, and the water's depth. Invasive plant species modify the natural plant community. Broadly speaking, aquatic plants can be thought of as emergent, floating-leaved, floating, or submersed.

- **Emergent plants,** such as cattail or bulrush, have their roots in mud beneath the water and stalks and leaves that extend above the water's surface. Many animals, such as waterfowl and muskrats, use emergent plants as habitat and food.

- **Floating-leaved plants,** such as pond lilies, water lilies, and watershield, are also rooted underwater but have leaves or flowers that float upon the water's surface.

- **Floating plants,** such as Common Duckweed, float entirely on the surface, with their roots dangling below and taking nutrients directly from the lake's water.

- **Submersed plants,** such as Eurasian water-milfoil or coontail, live entirely below the surface and have soft stems. You may have felt them tickling your toes while out for a dip.

Is there a difference between pond lilies and water lilies?

Pond lilies and water lilies are different aquatic plants of the Nymphaeaceae family. It's easiest to tell the difference between the two by their flowers. Both plants provide shade for creatures and regulate subsurface temperature on hot summer days.

Nuphar Polysepala, commonly known as pond lily, is indigenous to Vancouver Island.
PHOTO BY I, KENPEI

Pond lilies (*Nuphar polysepala*) The 4-6 sepals of a pond lily flower form a golden yellow cup. Pond lilies don't have the splash or colour of water lilies, but that doesn't mean they're not impressive. Pond lilies are indigenous to Vancouver Island and have been in regional lakes for thousands of years.

Nymphaea odorata, commonly known as a waterlily, is pretty, but not indigenous to Vancouver Island.
PHOTO BY NEIL DICKIE

Water lilies (*Nymphaea odorata*) Water lilies vary from white, pink, red, blue, to pale yellow, but never the same golden yellow as pond lilies. Water lily blossoms open during the day and close in the evening. They are not indigenous to Vancouver Island, and have usually been introduced for their aesthetic value.

Under the leaves of both pond lilies and water lilies are long underwater leaf stalks called petioles, which send nutrients down to tough underground structures in the lake bottom called rhizomes. In the winter, the rhizomes lie dormant, waiting to send up new shoots in the spring.

How do aquatic plants spread from one lake to another?

Invasive aquatic plants spread between lakes via watercraft such as canoes, kayaks, paddleboards, boats with electric motors, and associated equipment. A leaf stuck on the bottom of a boat can fall off into a different lake and establish itself there. After a day at the lake, always:

- **Clean** your boat and gear.
- **Drain** all water from your boat and gear onto land.
- **Dry** all parts of your boat and gear completely.

What ecological zones does a lake have?

In and around lakes there are many different ecological zones, which are interdependent and support different natural processes and species. These zones are largely based on water depth.

- The riparian zone is where the land meets the water, along the shoreline where wetlands are often found.
- The littoral zone includes the water close to the shore. With plenty of sunlight and warm water, this area supports aquatic plants and a wide diversity of animals and insects.
- The limnetic zone is out in the open water, from the surface down to eight meters below.
- The profundal zone is the water beyond the limnetic zone, beyond eight meters depth. Little light reaches this zone, meaning few plants can photosynthesize or make oxygen here. Many of Victoria's smaller lakes do not have a profundal zone, as they are too shallow.

- The benthic zone includes the surface of sediments at the bottom of a lake. Dragonflies and midges start their lives here, while western painted turtles join them in the winters, burrowed into the sediments.

What is trophic status?

Plants and algae support fish and insects in a lake, and nutrients such as nitrogen and phosphorus support plants and algae. Trophic status is a measure of the amount of nutrients in a lake.

- **Oligotrophic** lakes are poor in nutrients. They are deep and clear, with rocky shores and few rooted plants. Oligotrophic lakes do not produce many fish.

- **Eutrophic** lakes are rich in nutrients. They are green and weedy, have mucky shores and bottoms, and can be plagued by algae blooms. Eutrophic lakes produce lots of fish.

- **Mesotrophic** lakes are in the middle. They have more diverse aquatic life than oligotrophic lakes but are not as nutrient rich as eutrophic lakes.

The balance of nutrients in a lake changes over time. As they age, lakes slowly fill with sediments and organic matter, a natural process called eutrophication. Eutrophication can be greatly accelerated when additional nutrients enter a lake via runoff from lawns and streets, septic systems, or nearby agriculture.

Data on the trophic status for Victoria's lakes is limited, but reports published by the BC Lake Stewardship Society indicate that:

- Langford Lake has generally shown to be eutrophic,
- Prospect Lake, monitored from 1986–2011, was mesotrophic for 14 of those years and oligotrophic for the other 5, and
- Fork Lake was mesotrophic in 2000 and oligotrophic 2001–2006.

What are wetlands?

Wetlands are lands saturated by water for all or most of the year. All wetlands are essential to life and water quality, but not all wetlands are the same.

A **swamp** is a wetland that is forested, dominated by woody plants such as trees and shrubs. Swamps are often found along the shores of rivers or lakes and depend on water flowing through them to create natural fluctuations in the water level.

A **marsh** is a wetland dominated by emergent herbaceous (non-woody) plants like grasses, rushes, or reeds. Emergent plants are rooted underwater but have leaves or stems that reach out above the surface, such as cattails. Marshes are frequently or continually flooded and act as a shoreline transition between the aquatic and terrestrial ecosystems. Both swamps and marshes can have aquatic vegetation.

A **bog**, also known as a quagmire or muskeg, is a peat-depositing wetland that may or may not be connected to a lake or stream. Being fed mostly by rainwater or snow melt, bogs tend to have few nutrients and are acidic. Under these conditions, plants grow and decay slowly. Distinct species of plants and animals seek out bogs for their homes, and as such bogs provide pockets of exceptional biodiversity.

Fens are similar to bogs as they often have an abundance of peat, however, fens are able to support marsh-like vegetation such as sedges or wildflowers because they are often connected to slow moving water, meaning they will have more nutrients, and can therefore support different wetland species from a bog.

What is harmful to lakes?

Climate change, loss of habitat, invasive species, pollution, and human activity are all threats to lake ecosystems. None of these threats exist independently, and some of them enable others.

Pollution brings excess nutrients or pathogens into a lake, which impacts the broader ecosystem, leading to algae blooms and the loss of life in the lake. A variety of human activities pollute lakes, and some are a little less direct than you might expect.

Point source pollution is a direct outfall into a lake, such as a pipe carrying wastewater or a motorized boat leaking oil. Non-point source pollution exists over a lake's broader watershed and includes runoff of fertilized lawns, soap used to wash cars, storm water runoff, and seepage from septic systems.

Forestry operations impact lakes because forests absorb precipitation, and removing trees or plants causes increased inflows to a lake. This alters its shoreline and depth, while also adding more sediment and phosphorus to the water. When agriculture is improperly managed, nutrients and pathogens from manure can seep into a lake and livestock can damage shorelines.

Invasive species are also harmful to lakes. Bits of aquatic plants can catch on a boat and then establish themselves in a new lake when that boat is launched elsewhere. Introduced species of fish, frogs, or turtles can directly kill indigenous species or compete with them for food and habitat.

Even low-impact recreation such as swimming, hiking, or paddling can have an impact on lakes. Sunscreen, lotions, and hair products can dissolve in the water. Animals may seek out litter or may be frightened away from their water source due to human presence or noise such as music.

Are algae bad for lakes?

Algae are the foundation of a lake's ecosystem, as they are at the bottom of the food web. Tiny creatures such as zooplankton, aquatic insects, and fish fry use algae for shelter and food. Mammals, birds, fish, reptiles, and amphibians depend on those creatures as a source of food.

Algae are beautiful under a microscope. They feed on phosphorus and nitrogen and produce food through photosynthesis, getting their green colour from chlorophyl – just like grasses, ferns, and trees.

What is a blue-green algae bloom?

A blue-green algae bloom forms a scum or slime on a lake's surface, making the water look like pea soup. These blooms reduce oxygen in the water, block sunlight needed by aquatic plants, and are poisonous for fish, birds, amphibians, pets, and humans.

The surprising thing about blue-green algae, however, is that they are not actually algae. They are a type of bacteria known as cyanobacteria. Cyanobacteria are considered by some to be the oldest lifeforms on earth; they predate dinosaurs and are the force that turned dead plants into crude oil.

Many factors contribute to a blue-green algae bloom (and blooms occur naturally), however, the presence of too much phosphorus or sediment is often the triggering event.

Not all blooms are easy to see, and toxins can still be present even if the water looks fine. They usually happen in late summer or early fall but can occur at any time of year. A bloom can last from a few days to a few months.

Natural shorelines prevent algae blooms, as they filter out nutrients and sediment before they get into the water.

Does climate change affect lakes?

Weather patterns and trends are changing over time. The earth is warming, and this will cause many natural systems to break down or change irreversibly. Canada's freshwater lakes are under threat from climate change.

The lakes themselves are getting hotter – in fact, the world's lakes are warming quicker than its oceans or atmosphere. Northern lakes in particular are seeing the most dramatic increases in temperature.

Even small changes in climate affect fish and microscopic plants, which can have a cascading effect on lake ecosystems. Warmer water, lower snowfall, and hotter summers provide perfect growing conditions for toxic algae blooms, while loss of forests due to forestry or wildfire impacts the ground's ability to absorb water, leading to flooding and changes in watersheds.

Who owns a lake?

There have been many legal challenges to the question of who owns a particular lake, but in general lakes are considered public resources. While a person or a company can buy land that surrounds a lake, they usually do not own the lake itself or the things inside it.

Different levels of government regulate lakes. The federal government regulates what happens on a lake's surface, such as boating, while the provincial government is responsible for the bottom of a lake and its water column (the water itself).

For lakes in public parks, such as Matheson Lake, a regional government such as the Capital Regional District regulates parkland, while a local government such as the District of Metchosin regulates lands outside the park that are part of the watershed. Decisions made hundreds of kilometers away from a lake can impact its health.

Can anyone visit a lake?

Access to lakes and along waterways such as creek beds or rivers is a complex legal question, with different laws applying in different parts of Canada.

While lakes themselves are generally considered public resources, the land surrounding a lake can be privately owned, and the owner of that land can restrict public access. Likewise, roads can also be privately owned. This largely prevents access to many, if not most, of the lakes on Vancouver Island.

Access to the outdoors is a big issue on Vancouver Island, and it should be. While the island is known and loved for its wilderness, much of the land beyond Victoria is owned or managed by forestry companies, which often prevent access to reduce vandalism, liability, or the risk of forest fires.

In many European countries the "right to roam" is a generally accepted, legally mandated principle, but it does not exist in British Columbia. If you would like more access to the outdoors, you need to influence government and get involved with local advocacy groups. Write to your member of parliament and join one of groups listed in the acknowledgements section of this book.

How are lakes named?

The name of a lake often reveals its history (Quarantine Lake), unique natural features (Grass Lake), animals that live nearby (Elk/Beaver Lake), its shape (Spectacle Lake), or what it is used for (Quarry Lake).

Most lakes near Victoria take their names from people (Langford Lake), and a few seem to be named after animals but are actually named for people (Pike Lake and Eagles Lake). Some lakes are named after military boats (Thetis Lake), and some just have numbers for their names (Second Lake).

In British Columbia the names of geographic places, including lakes, are assigned by the provincial government. Place names change, however, and communities often define their own names for places. Names such as Lookout Lake or Mary Lake are not listed in the province's geographic registry of place names.

Most of Victoria's lakes have had multiple names given to them by colonial settlers since they started arriving a few hundred years ago. Yet Indigenous people have lived on Vancouver Island for much longer and have their own place names. Many locals now refer to local landmarks, such as Mount Doug, by their Indigenous place name, in this case, PKOLS.

Place names are fascinating and powerful. Nondescript names, such as Site C, can obscure the true nature or context of a place, which can impact public interest in them.

Who protects lakes?

The short answer: you.

Protecting a lake involves more than just the people who live on its shores or visit it for recreation. Everyone and everything that is part of the watershed can impact a lake, and therefore it takes the efforts of many to ensure our lakes are healthy.

Lakes fall under a patchwork of legislation, and as such different governments monitor their health. However, it is usually organized groups of volunteers that save lakes in times of crisis, such as potential changes in ownership or developments upstream.

Volunteers also prevent problems from happening in the first place through proactive maintenance. They monitor water quality, remove invasive species, build trails, and sound the alarm when something is out of balance.

Do your part and get involved with a local community organization.

Hike

The Victoria area offers many opportunities for hikers to get off the beaten track. With many provincial, regional, municipal and community parks sharing borders, there are some great day hikes that include a stop at a lake or two. Here are a few ideas.

Always hike with a friend, as it is easy to get lost and even a twisted ankle can leave you stranded. Encounters with wildlife such as bears, cougars, and wolves can happen in the Victoria area. Cell reception is poor or does not exist on some of the hikes described in this book, so always leave a trip plan with someone you trust.

Always pack the ten essentials for your hike:

- paper maps and a compass, offline GPS maps as a backup
- enough food for one extra day
- water and a way to treat it such as a filter or tablets
- sun protection: sunscreen, hat, and sunglasses
- insulation: extra layers and dry clothes
- lights such as a headlamp, with spare batteries
- first-aid supplies: bandages, blister dressings, and a splint
- fire starter: waterproof matches or a lighter
- repair kit: multi-tool, scissors, duct tape, and pliers
- emergency shelter: high visibility emergency blanket.

Walk

Simply being close to water is therapeutic for many. Whether you are looking to share an afternoon with a friend, a picnic with the family, or for space to pause and reflect, lakes and their surroundings are a great destination. Here are a few good places for walks.

- **Florence Lake** p. 110
- **Poirier Lake** p. 173
- **Blinkhorn Lake** p. 140
- **Durrance Lake** p. 30
- **Fork Lake** p 66
- **Thetis Lake** p. 82
- **Langford Lake** p. 98
- **Elk/Beaver Lake** p. 24
- **Swan Lake** p. 50
- **Mary Lake** p. 77

Be sure to stay on the trails, share trails with others, respect private property, and use headphones if you want to listen to music. Never walk on a frozen lake or river unless there are signs clearly saying it is safe to do so.

If you are taking a four-legged friend with you on your walk, be sure to know when dogs are allowed to be off-leash. Dogs also need to stay on trails to minimize disturbance to the plants and animals who live at the lake.

Swim

Swimming outdoors adds a whole new element to being "out there."
The Pacific Ocean is often too cold for swimming, but Victoria has many
freshwater lakes for swimmers and sunbathers alike. Really want to know
a lake? Bring your snorkel! Here are some favourite swimming holes.

Swimming can impact lake ecosystems. Suntan lotion, perfume, urine, and
animal feces can have negative impacts on water quality. Wildlife such as
sunning turtles can be frightened or deprived of their natural habitat with
humans in their space. Please swim responsibly.

Swimming has its own level of risk, so know your limits and stay within
them. Blue-green algae blooms, *E. coli,* and high levels of bacteria do
occur in the Victoria area and are harmful for humans and pets, so watch
for any signage on site. The Vancouver Island Health Authority monitors
the quality of water for swimming at Victoria's lakes and provides regular
beach reports through their website.

Fish

It's hard to beat the simplicity and peace of freshwater fishing, be it from shore, a float tube, or a kayak. Here are some of Victoria's hotspots for trout and bass.

A valid BC Freshwater Fishing Licence is needed for anglers in BC. Licenses can be purchased online from the Province, or in-person at some retailers and outfitters. Different regulations apply to various waterways and species – be sure you know these regulations and comply with them.

Knowing when to fish is a matter of knowing how seasons impact fish – specifically their food and the water temperature. For example, it's useful to know that insects begin hatching in the spring, trout like cooler water, and bass like warmer water. By putting these pieces together, expect the following in the Victoria area:

- **March to June:** rainbow and cutthroat trout
- **June to August:** smallmouth bass
- **September to October:** rainbow and cutthroat trout

Paddle

Being off shore, quietly gliding along the water's surface is one of the best ways to explore lakes, watch wildlife, and admire seasonal changes along the shoreline. Here are some of Victoria's best lakes for paddling.

- **Spectacle Lake**   p. 124
- **Thetis Lake**   p. 82
- **Matheson Lake**   p. 134
- **Durrance Lake**   p. 30
- **Langford Lake**   p. 98

- **Prospect Lake**   p. 38
- **Glen Lake**   p. 104
- **Elk/Beaver Lake**   p. 24
- **Kemp Lake**   p. 170
- **Blinkhorn Lake**   p. 140

Unexpected events can happen when you are paddling, and sometimes it can be hard to get out of the water if required. Take appropriate safety training, know your limits, and wear a lifejacket.

After your lake visit, remove any fragments of aquatic vegetation from your vessel and let it dry for about five days before going back in the water. This prevents the spread of invasive species like Eurasian water-milfoil and water fleas.

- **Clean plants, animals, and mud from your boat and gear.**
- **Drain all water from your boat and gear onto land.**
- **Dry all parts of your boat and gear completely.**

Bike

There's simply no better way to arrive at a lake than by bike. With plenty of cycling routes, Victoria offers many opportunities for cyclists in search of a lake destination. Here are some great day trips.

Plan your route ahead of time to take advantage of Victoria's many multiuse trails. Take a bike skills course to ensure your safety while riding, particularly when using the roads.

When cycling off-road, always stay on well-defined trails. Your weight is concentrated on a smaller surface with bike tires than with feet, and cycling can harm earthen trails. Grass, fields, meadows, exposed tree roots and trails are particularly vulnerable to bike tires during the wetter seasons.

Families

People of all ages enjoy the many pursuits that lakes offer. From beaches to playgrounds and picnic areas, here are some lakes that will delight the whole family.

- **Langford Lake** p. 118
- **Glen Lake** p. 104
- **Spectacle Lake** p. 124
- **Matheson Lake** p. 134
- **Poirier Lake** p. 173
- **Prospect Lake** p .38
- **Lake Ida Anne** p. 115
- **Swan Lake** p. 50
- **Eagles Lake** p. 74
- **Thetis Lake** p. 82

Swan Lake has a nature house with programming offered throughout the year, Elk/Beaver Lake has a seasonal nature house, and Mary Lake has a nature house available to visit on request. The YMCA offers outdoor programs at Glinz Lake, and local scouting events are held at Young Lake. Facilities can be rented for groups staying overnight at both Glinz Lake and Young Lake.

Remember, children are naturally curious, and getting lost or drowning are serious risks. Never leave children unattended and ensure that those who can't swim wear a lifejacket near the water.

Accessibility

Everyone deserves to experience nature. Fortunately, there are many lakes in the Victoria area with accessible trails, parking, toilets, playgrounds, and picnic tables. Here are some lakes recommended for anyone with reduced mobility.

- **Glen Lake**   p. 104
- **Durrance Lake**   p. 30
- **Poirier Lake**   p. 173
- **Fork Lake**   p. 66
- **Florence Lake**   p. 110

- **Elk/Beaver Lake**   p. 24
- **Lake Ida Anne**   p. 115
- **Blenkinsop Lake**   p. 56
- **Mary Lake**   p. 77
- **Swan Lake**   p. 50

Trail conditions and infrastructure can change. Fortunately, this is usually for the better, but always be prepared for things to be different from expected when you arrive. Take a friend if you can.

Saanich Peninsula

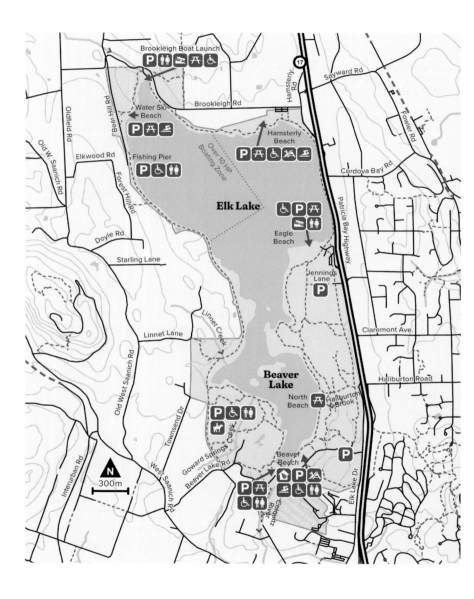

Elk/Beaver Lake

Watershed: Colquitz River

Elevation: 65 m

Surface: 181.6 ha

Perimeter: 6.7 km

Max Depth: 19 m

Access: Elk/Beaver Lake Regional Park (Hamsterly Road for Hamsterly Beach, Jennings Lane for Eagle Beach, Beaver Lake Road for Beaver Beach, or Bear Hill Road for Water Ski Beach)

Elk/Beaver Lake is often a visitor's first impression of Vancouver Island as they glimpse its sparkling blue waters from the Patricia Bay Highway. With sand beaches, playgrounds, a boat launch, a fishing pier, an equestrian centre, a nature house, and a 10 km walking trail, Elk/Beaver Lake has something for everyone – to which the nearly 1.6 million yearly visitors can attest!

The lake and surrounding wetlands attract birds such as mergansers, buffleheads, mallards, geese, and eagles, so bring your binoculars. The vegetation along the shoreline has also been known to provide homes for river otters, indigenous (and endangered) western painted turtles, and introduced red-eared slider turtles.

Beaches & Swimming

There are four family-friendly sand beaches at Elk/Beaver Lake: Hamsterly Beach, Eagle Beach, Beaver Beach, and Water Ski Beach.

Hamsterly Beach on the north side is a large, accessible sand beach with picnic tables and a playground. With plenty of sunshine, it is perfect for swimmers and picnickers of all ages. On the south side, Beaver Beach also offers a playground, picnic tables, and a seasonal nature house.

Water Ski Beach is not recommended for swimming due to powerboats in the area. Blue-green algae blooms have occurred frequently at Elk/Beaver Lake in recent years. These blooms are toxic for humans and pets, so watch for signage on site.

Elk/Beaver Lake.
PHOTO BY ERNIE DICKEY

Hikes & Walks

The 10 km trail around the lake is considered easy and takes about 2.5 hours to complete, leading through forests of Douglas fir and western red cedar. Watch for bald eagles and osprey hunting for fish in the lake.

Fishing

Elk/Beaver Lake is a popular place to fish and is stocked regularly with Blackwater River and Fraser Valley strains of rainbow trout. Expect to find catchable rainbow and cutthroat trout, as well as introduced smallmouth and largemouth bass, pumpkinseed sunfish, yellow perch, common carp, and brown bullhead.

Use the trail system to find numerous shore fishing opportunities or launch a boat to cast from the lake's surface. The fishing pier on the west side has provided good bass fishing (orange powerbait is a good bet). Beaver lake is much shallower than Elk Lake and has a fair amount more weeds, so take that into account when deciding on the type of fish you are looking to catch.

Paddling & Boats

Being the largest lake in the area, Elk/Beaver Lake is naturally a favourite for paddlers of all sorts, and even windsurfers. If you are paddling, launch at Beaver Beach and admire the dragonflies and vegetation along the shorelines and islands nearby. A variety of rowing programs are offered for athletes of all ages at Eagle Beach by the Victoria City Rowing Club, which also hosts regattas and other local rowing competitions.

For larger boats, launches are available at Brookleigh Boat Launch and Eagle Beach. Vessels over 10 horsepower are permitted only in the northwest corner of Elk Lake. Power vessels towing water-skiers or equipment are prohibited between sunrise and 11:00 am. Remember that water levels fluctuate, so watch for submerged stumps near the shore.

Cycling

The best route for cyclists to Elk/Beaver Lake is via the Lochside Trail and Sayward Road. Within the park, cycling is permitted on multi-use trails only. Bike racks are provided at Hamsterly Beach, Eagle Beach, Beaver Beach, the Filter Beds, and the fishing pier.

Accessibility

Hamsterly Beach offers great lake access for wheelchair users, with accessible parking, picnic tables, and washrooms. Likewise, Eagle Beach offers accessible washrooms and parking. Most of the 10 km lakeside trail is flat, wide, and well-groomed, with views of the lake interspersed throughout. A highlight is the fishing pier on the west side, featuring accessible parking, washrooms, and the pier itself.

Parking, Washrooms, and Dogs

All beaches and the fishing pier offer accessible parking and toilets, except for Water Ski Beach which offers only basic parking. The Brookleigh Boat Launch and the Filter Beds have basic parking and accessible toilets.

Dogs must be under control and on trails. Dogs are not permitted on the beaches between June 1 and September 15 except to pass through on a leash. Watch for signage regarding blue-green algae blooms, which are toxic for pets.

Creeks & Watershed

Elk/Beaver Lake is the headwaters of the Colquitz River. Four named creeks are inflows: Whiskey Creek (Hamsterly Creek), Haliburton Brook, Linnet Creek, and O'Donnel Creek. The main outflow is the Colquitz River at the south end of Beaver Lake. The Colquitz River leads southwards through Saanich and ultimately drains into Portage Inlet at the northern end of the Gorge Waterway.

Local History

Elk Lake once served as Victoria's primary water supply. In 1864 the Spring Ridge Water Company laid log pipes to transport water from Elk Lake to downtown Victoria. Families would either go downtown to fill their water barrels, or have the water delivered to them by horse and wagon. In 1875 water from Elk Lake began to be piped directly to Victoria homes.

The city grew quickly, so the level of Beaver Lake was raised in 1895 to connect it with Elk Lake, thereby increasing the water supply. The current name of Elk/Beaver Lake serves as a reminder that this lake was once two separate bodies of water. Pieces of this era can still be seen in the double track trail on the west side of the lake, which used to be part of the route of the Victoria and Sidney (V&S) railway from 1894 to 1919.

As one might expect, Elk and Beaver Lakes were named after animals. While elk are not present on the Saanich Peninsula today, they can still be found farther north on Vancouver Island. Beavers are still present in Saanich, and beaver dams caused flooding at (you guessed it) Beaver Lake as recently as 2013. Hamsterly Beach likely takes its name from the Hamsterly Farm, which was famous for its strawberry jam in the early 1900s.

The Beaver Lake Store, which once operated at 4808 West Saanich Road, started as a small confectionery on the east side of the road. When their landlord raised the rent, cousins Eulalie and Marie Harrison literally hauled the building across the street.

Skulls of an extinct type of bison, *Bison antiquus*, have been found near Elk Lake by archaeologists working with the Royal British Columbia Museum. The skulls have been radiocarbon-dated to over 11,000 years old.

Dragonflies

Dragonflies are a particular delight to see buzzing around Victoria's lakes in the summer. Their colours are vibrant, and with four wings their flight is as mesmerising as it is versatile; dragonflies can fly straight up or down, hover in mid air, or change direction without turning their bodies. To add to these already impressive features, they don't bite humans and they devour mosquitos. It's pretty hard not to like dragonflies!

Few people know that dragonflies spend the majority of their lives underwater. They come out of lakes after a long metamorphosis (sometimes several years) and spend only a few months above the surface. While they are living underwater, dragonfly larvae eat anything smaller than themselves, including other insects, tadpoles, and even small fish. And yes, dragonfly larvae eat mosquito larvae too.

To some extent, the altitude of a lake affects what kinds of dragonflies you'll find near it, as higher lakes generally have colder water, which is better for some species than others. Altitude, and the associated climate, also affects the type of vegetation that lines the shores of a lake. The warmer freshwater marshes of Victoria are ideal places to look for a bounty of dragonflies in the summer.

Dragonflies are thought to have been on earth for over 300 million years. Their ancestors, known as meganisoptera, are the largest known insects to rule our skies, with wingspans of up to 75 cm.

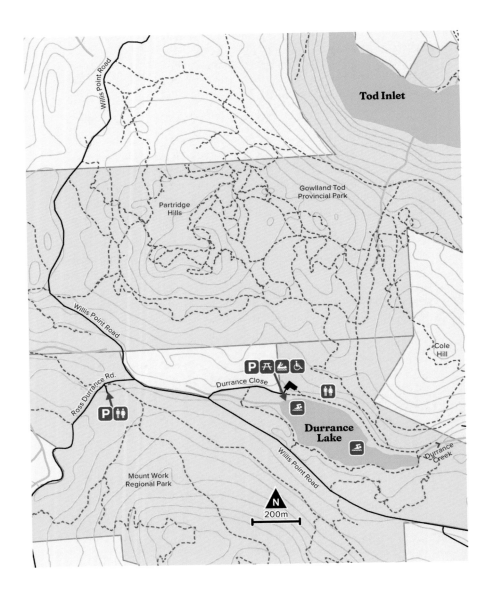

Tod Inlet

Gowlland Tod
Provincial Park

Partridge
Hills

Willis Point Road

Cole
Hill

Ross Durrance Rd.

Durrance Close

Durrance
Lake

Durrance
Creek

Willis Point Road

Mount Work
Regional Park

N
200m

Durrance Lake

Watershed: Tod Creek

Elevation: 134 m

Surface: 7.6 ha

Perimeter: 1.4 km

Max Depth: 16 m

Access: Mount Work Regional Park (Willis Point Road)

Durrance Lake is one of the best places to soak up sun, swim, fish, and enjoy a lake atmosphere in the Victoria area. Carry-in boats are welcome, a walking trail circles the lake, and plenty of opportunities for hiking and mountain biking are close by. Durrance Lake is the largest lake in Mount Work Regional Park and is an ideal place for people of all ages to spend a summer afternoon.

A variety of trees can be found along the lakeside trail, including arbutus, grand fir, Douglas fir, red alder, and cedar. If you are walking the lake trail in late March, watch for western white trillium, a white flower with three petals that turns pink or purple as it reaches the end of its lifespan in May. With the lack of wind in the area, these flowers rely on the hardworking ants below to find new homes for their seeds.

The lake and surrounding area has been known to provide homes for birds such as Steller's jay, woodpeckers, and hummingbirds, feeding on insects and berries produced by the surrounding ecosystem.

Beaches & Swimming

The main sand beach is a short walk (300 m) from the parking lot on the north shore. Expect to find an easy, shallow entry to the water and a beautiful view of the lake with Mount Work in the background. For those seeking a more secluded space to swim, there are many other access points around the shore of the lake, including the occasional fallen log.

Hikes & Walks

For walkers, an easy-to-moderate 2 km trail circles the lake, leading through an impressive forest on the south side. Starting from the northern side, the trail is well-groomed, flat, open, and wide. An unmarked trail branches off a bit past the main beach, which leads into

Durrance Lake.
PHOTO BY MURRAY SHARRATT

unmarked and unmaintained trails in the neighbouring Gowlland Tod Provincial Park.

Continuing around to the south side of the lake, the trail becomes a shady single-track, rooty, and sometimes rocky. Here the trees go right to the water's edge. You'll know you are close to finishing the loop when you cross a small wooden boardwalk over an unnamed creek on the west side of the lake.

For those looking for a greater challenge, less than a kilometer west of Durrance Lake is the northern trailhead for the impressive Summit Trail, which leads past glacial rock formations and a grove of arbutus trees to the top of Mount Work. At 449 meters high, Mount Work is the highest point on the Saanich Peninsula and offers panoramic views.

The Summit Trail is considered moderate to challenging, so bring a friend, proper clothes, a lunch, and water. Continuing down the south side of Mount Work will take you to the quiet Fork Lake in the heart of the District of Highlands.

Fishing at Durrance Lake in the fall.
PHOTO BY ADAM UNGSTAD

Fishing

A favourite for fly fishing, Durrance Lake has been stocked since the 1920s. Expect to find coastal cutthroat trout, rainbow trout, and smallmouth bass. Catchable Fraser Valley rainbow trout are generally released in the spring and fall, and coastal cutthroat trout were released for the first time in over a decade in June 2019.

The north and east sides of the lake are the best for shoreline casting. The east side is a good area to try for bass during spawning season, with its fallen logs and aquatic vegetation, but mind the turtles. Still fishing with brightly coloured artificial eggs near the bottom has been successful with trout at this lake. There is a fishing pier and a boat launch close to the parking lot.

Paddling & Boats

A car-top boat launch is accessible from the parking lot. Electric motors only. While there's lots of activity on the shores of Durrance Lake, getting out to the middle is a peaceful pleasure.

Cycling

For experienced road cyclists, consider arriving at Durrance Lake via the narrow, winding, and shady roads in the District of Highlands. Start with either Munn Road or Millstream Lake Road, then follow Ross Durrance Road. Watch for a glimpse of Pease Lake on your approach to Durrance Lake, and after a swim make it a loop by returning via Willis Point Road and the Interurban Trail.

For mountain bikers, the legendary Partridge Hills are directly to the north of the lake. There is also a designated mountain biking area on the eastern side of Mount Work Park.

Accessibility

Accessible toilets and picnic tables are available near the parking lot. The gravel path along the north side of the lake is well-groomed and level, offering easy access to the fishing pier and main beach, and views of the lake with Mount Work in the background. The trail on the southern side of the lake is not recommended anyone with reduced mobility or strollers.

The fishing dock at Durrance Lake.
PHOTO BY ADAM UNGSTAD

Parking, Washrooms, and Dogs

The main parking is found on Durrance Close, which branches off Willis Point Road. Toilets are available on the northern side of the lake. Dogs must be under control and on the trail, and are not allowed on beaches or picnic areas between June 1 and September 15, except to pass through on a leash.

Creeks & Watershed

Durrance Lake is part of the Tod Creek Watershed. Water leaves Durrance Lake via Durrance Creek, which then connects with Heal Creek before joining Tod Creek, and ultimately makes its way northwards, emptying into Tod Inlet.

Local History

The City of Victoria acquired the land around Durrance Lake in 1960 from BC Electric via a trade; the city received 204 acres around Durrance Lake in exchange for 105 acres directly north of Thetis Lake. BC Electric needed the land to build power lines into the city. This area is now known as the Pike Lake Substation.

If you have trouble spelling the word "Durrance" you're not the only one – the name of this lake has a history of different spellings. Named after pioneering settlers in the area, the name was first recorded as "Durant" by the Geological Survey in 1911, followed by "Durants" on Hibben's Map in 1929, "Durrant" by the BC Gazetteer in 1930, and finally as "Durrance" in 1934 by the Saanich Municipality.

Did you know?

Surprisingly, Durrance Lake is not in the District of Saanich as is often thought, nor in the neighbouring District of Highlands.

Rather, Durrance Lake is part of the Juan de Fuca Electoral Area (JdFEA), which stretches along the west side of Vancouver Island, from the community of Otter Point (just beyond Sooke) to Port Renfrew.

Western painted turtles

Spend time near Victoria's lakes between April and September, and before long you'll see a group of freshwater turtles sunning themselves on a log protruding from the water. These turtles aren't simply working on their tan like you are – rather, they rely on the sun's warmth for their bodies to function properly. So find your own place to bask and leave them be.

Indigenous to Vancouver Island are *Chrysemys picta bellii*, commonly known as western painted turtles. These turtles have red on their underside (called plastrons), are omnivorous, and have sharp, hooked beaks. Much like birds, turtles have beaks but no teeth. Unfortunately, western painted turtles are endangered. The loss of natural shorelines, increased recreational use, roads, raccoons, and free-roaming pets all threaten their survival.

Several other turtle species are found in Victoria's lakes, including slider turtles, some of which are likely abandoned pets. Introduced turtles threaten indigenous species by competing for limited resources such as food and yes, places to bask in the sun.

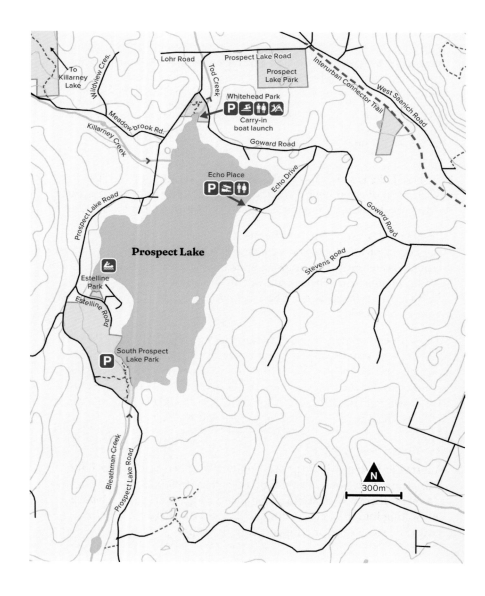

Prospect Lake

Watershed: Tod Creek

Max Depth: 14 m

Elevation: 48 m

Surface: 67.8 ha

Perimeter: 4.8 km

Access: Whitehead Park (Goward Road), Echo Place Boat Launch, South Prospect Lake Park (Prospect Lake Road), or Estelline Park (Estelline Road).

Prospect Lake is a recreational treasure in the heart of rural Saanich. While most of the shoreline has been claimed by private residences, three parks provide access to the water, as well as a launch for boat trailers.

On the north (sunny) end is Whitehead Park, which features a playground, picnic tables, and a swimming wharf. The District of Saanich has recently added new equipment to the playground and significant efforts have been made by the Friends of Tod Creek Watershed to restore the creek bed that borders the park, which is the start of Tod Creek.

The south end of the lake holds the larger, more secluded South Prospect Lake Park. A short, sometimes steep or rocky trail leads through trees to a view of the lake below. Watch for birds such as chickadees, nuthatches, sparrows, and flickers on your way. Also on the west side of the lake is the tiny Estelline Park, with a green space and access suitable to launch carry-in boats. There is a small island in the lake and several natural bays.

Beaches & Swimming

Whitehead Park provides the best family atmosphere at Prospect Lake, with plenty of sun and a swimming wharf that stretches beyond the grassy lakeshore. There's no sand beach, but plenty of grass to spread a blanket on. Getting into the water at South Prospect Lake Park will require navigating some steep and slippery rock outcrops.

The dock at Prospect Lake's Whitehead Park.
PHOTO BY ADAM UNGSTAD

Hikes & Walks

Given that most of the shoreline is privately owned, the trails at Prospect Lake are short strolls. South Prospect Lake Park provides an easy but sometimes steep or rocky path through forest to the water's edge. A short nature trail has also been created by the Friends of Tod Creek Watershed at Whitehead Park on the east side of Tod Creek.

For further walking and hiking opportunities in the area investigate the trails near Killarney Lake to the west or Fork Lake via Munn Road.

Fishing

Prospect Lake is popular for fishing of all sorts. It is known to be a reliable place to fish for smallmouth bass and is stocked regularly with rainbow trout. Coastal cutthroat, prickly sculpin, brown catfish, and pumpkinseed sunfish can be found as well.

There are few opportunities to cast from shore, so it's best to have a boat or a float tube for this one. The southeast corner of the lake is the deepest. Expect a decent chironomid hatch in the spring.

Paddling & Boats

There is a launch for boat trailers at Echo Place. Watch for signs on site indicating applicable regulations for motorized boats and activities such as waterskiing or tubing. Carry-in boats are best launched from Whitehead Park or the quieter Estelline Park.

Cycling

The most bike-friendly route to Prospect Lake is to take the Galloping Goose Regional Trail to where it intersects with Interurban Road, and then follow Interurban Trail to the north side of lake. Panama Flats offers an interesting detour along this route. An alternative is to take the Goose as far as Burnside Road West and follow it to Prospect Lake Road, which runs along the west side of the lake.

Accessibility

Whitehead Park offers parking close to the lake, with a pleasant view from the shore a short distance away via level, wheelchair accessible paths. The trails at South Prospect Lake Park are not wheelchair accessible.

Parking, Washrooms, and Dogs

The best parking is at Whitehead Park, although limited parking is available at the other access points. Seasonal toilets are generally available between May and November at Whitehead Park and Echo Place. Dogs must be under control at all access points and on a leash within 10 meters of the playground at Whitehead Park.

Creeks & Watershed

Prospect Lake is part of the Tod Creek Watershed. There are five named creeks that flow into Prospect Lake: Echo Creek, Mutter Brook, Bleathman Creek, Gibson Creek, and Killarney Creek. Tod Creek on the

Sunset fishing at Prospect Lake.
PHOTO BY MURRAY SHARRATT

northern shore is the main outflow, and water then continues north to Tod Inlet (an extension of Brentwood Bay).

Local History

Prospect Lake likely took its name from the "forty-niners" (a reference to the year 1849), who came from California in search of gold. While there is no evidence that gold was ever found in the area, the name Prospect Lake stuck even after the prospectors moved on.

Whitehead Park is named after the Whitehead family, who sold the land to Saanich in 1959. Herbert Thomas Whitehead was an architect from England who designed an elaborate house at the corner of Cook Street and Dallas Road in Victoria. The house, built in 1913, is now an elegant Bed and Breakfast known as the Dashwood Manor.

The community of Prospect Lake has a rich history full of stories and fascinating trivia. For more information about the history of the lake, find a copy of *Reflections on Prospect Lake*, a book produced by the Prospect Lake Heritage Society in 2012.

Did you know?

One of the first settlers of Prospect Lake was On Hing, a hard-working Chinese man who arrived in 1858 and owned 89 acres of land on the southeast side of the lake. On Hing, his wife, and family planted strawberries and fruit orchards over most of their land.

On Hing was known as a happy individual who travelled around the countryside with a wagon full of produce and chickens, trading for fresh meat, grain, and other supplies. Other than the work done cultivating their land and raising their family, little is known about On Hing's wife.

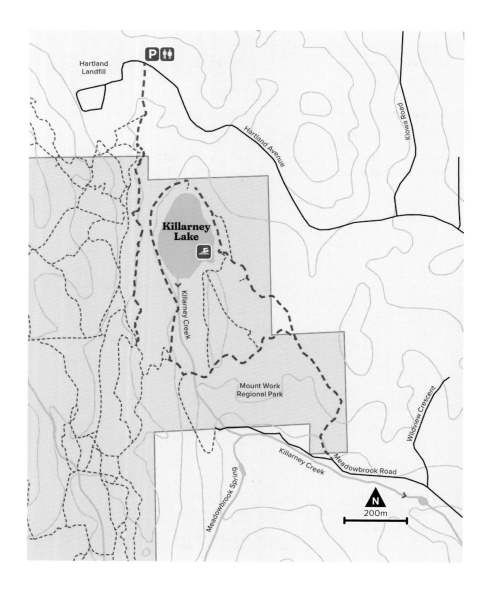

Killarney Lake

Watershed: Tod Creek

Perimeter: 0.7 km

Elevation: 107 m

Max Depth: 5 m

Surface: 3.4 ha

Access: Mount Work Regional Park (Hartland Avenue or Meadowbrook Road)

Killarney Lake has two distinct sides, and people approaching the lake from different directions will see two very different lakes.

Approaching from the south by the trail at the end of Meadowbrook Road is a unique, almost fairy-tale experience. The rural road leads past farms and cabins before it becomes a walking trail at the end. There is no parking here, so plan to arrive by bike or on foot.

After a 15-minute uphill walk you will come to a picture-perfect clearing on the shore of Killarney Lake, ideal for a picnic, with shimmering waters just below. On a quiet afternoon in the fall this approach is quite a beautiful experience.

Approaching Killarney Lake from the north, however, yields a different perspective. From the start, parking at Hartland leaves you acutely aware of just how close this lake is to the regional landfill. Making your way to the lake, your view is of power lines rather than indigenous forest and undergrowth. Once you arrive at the lake the first thing you may encounter (depending which way you go) is private property – despite maps that seem to show the lake falling entirely within Mount Work Regional Park.

Whether you choose to arrive by bike or foot from the south, or by car from the west, Killarney Lake is brimming with life and a fantastic place to spend time with friends. The lake is an absolute treasure to those who know about it.

Beaches & Swimming

There is no sand beach at Killarney Lake, but you can expect to find easy access to the water (you'll need to step over a few roots). Enjoy!

Hikes & Walks

Access from Meadowbrook Road is an enjoyable, uphill walk that takes about 15 minutes to get to the lake. There are numerous other hiking trails surrounding the lake in Mount Work Regional Park. The lake is popular in the summer, so walking is at its best in other seasons.

Fishing

There are no records of Killarney Lake being stocked with trout. With minimal parking, a bit of a walk to get in from either direction, and natural shorelines, you will likely want to cast from shore or bring a float-tube rather than a car-top boat.

Paddling & Boats

It is a significant effort to launch a canoe or a kayak here. As this is a smaller lake, you will be better off using something inflatable or a stand-up paddleboard.

Cycling

There are multiple cycling routes to get to Killarney Lake, the best being the Interurban Trail via the Galloping Goose Regional Trail. Cycling is not permitted on the trail from Meadowbrook Road. Mount Work is a favourite for mountain bikers, and the Hartland parking lot has a bike wash station.

Accessibility

The trail from Meadowbrook Road is well-groomed and wide, but the grade is too steep for wheelchairs. The route from Hartland is not recommended for people with limited mobility. Getting in the water will require careful footing. A more accessible alternative nearby is Durrance Lake.

Swan Lake

Watershed: Colquitz River

Perimeter: 1.2 km

Elevation: 12 m

Max Depth: 7 m

Surface: 9 ha

Access: Swan Lake Christmas Hill Nature Sanctuary (Swan Lake Road)

Swan Lake is nestled inside a thriving nature sanctuary in Victoria's suburban backyard, known as the Swan Lake Christmas Hill Nature Sanctuary. The nature house is an asset to the community, a living classroom that provides opportunities to discover and understand indigenous plants and animals. It features an impressive reading room, a indigenous plant garden, and a wide variety of interpretive and educational programs for all ages and interests.

The shores of Swan Lake are a marshy habitat with cattails and duckweed providing food and refuge for many species of waterfowl and other residents such as muskrats, river otters, and mink. The trees surrounding the lake are inhabited by wrens, warblers, and other songbirds. The northern harrier, a slim, long-tailed hawk, can sometimes be seen hunting over the marsh.

Of course, where there are birds, there must be insects. Buzzing across the water and through the marsh of Swan Lake are damselflies, dragonflies, water beetles, and water striders. These insects also provide food for the resident newts and frogs.

In addition to the fauna of the lake, you'll find unique flora and fungi. Look for Garry oak, arbutus, and Douglas fir trees, along with some of the oldest heritage cottonwood trees in the region.

When the warm summer weather passes, Swan Lake is also a great place to be after a snowfall, where you can find tracks in the snow left by critters such as muskrats and mink.

Swan Lake.
PHOTO BY ERNIE DICKEY

Beaches & Swimming

There are no beaches at Swan Lake and swimming is not permitted. The lake and surrounding area are designated as a nature sanctuary, and as such the water is reserved as a refuge for waterfowl. Wetlands surround the lake, resulting in a muddy bottom that would be unpleasant for swimming.

Hikes & Walks

The 2.5 km trail around the lake and surrounding marsh takes about 45 minutes to walk, with the unique highlight being a floating boardwalk a short distance from the nature house. On your walk, notice the shape of the surrounding hills and the vegetation that inhabits the marshes, which indicate that the lake used to be larger than its current form.

If you're looking for a longer walk, visit the Garry oak preserve on the nearby Christmas Hill, where you'll find butterflies and wildflowers in the right season and vistas of the surrounding area year-round.

Fishing

Swan Lake has a history of eutrophication (an overabundance of nutrients), which has resulted in a low fish population. As such, fishing is not currently permitted. As the lake returns to equilibrium, coastal cutthroat trout coming up the Colquitz River may begin to re-establish themselves in the lake.

Paddling & Boats

Boats or paddle boards are not permitted on Swan Lake.

Cycling

Cycling is not permitted on trails in the sanctuary, but you can get there on a bike via the Lochside Regional Trail, a short distance from the intersection with the Galloping Goose Regional Trail at the Switch Bridge. If you'd like to visit the nature house, exit the Lochside at Darwin Ave, go through the municipal parking lot, and follow the quieter roads along the west perimeter of the sanctuary. Bike racks are available at the nature house.

Accessibility

The nature house, washrooms, viewing dock, floating boardwalk, and some trails are all wheelchair accessible. The entire lake loop can be more challenging than expected and is not possible for wheelchairs.

Parking, Washrooms, and Dogs

The main parking lot is found at Swan Lake Road, a short distance from the nature house, which has public washrooms during open hours. Dogs are not permitted in the nature sanctuary to minimize disturbance of the indigenous species who call it home.

Creeks & Watershed

Swan Lake is part of the sprawling Colquitz River Watershed. Water enters Swan Lake via Blenkinsop Creek on the east side and leaves via Swan Creek on the west side before joining the Colquitz River, eventually emptying into Portage Inlet (at the northern end of the Gorge Waterway).

While its location makes Swan Lake accessible for an afternoon stroll, human settlement around the lake hasn't been without drawbacks. Swan Lake has previously been under threat from run-off and other forms of human pollution from the nearby hills. In response, the nature sanctuary is actively involved in restoration activities for this valuable urban ecosystem.

Local History

Swan Lake has a history in hospitality. In 1864 the Swan Lake Hotel was constructed on its south side. Guests could fish in the summer, skate in the winter, and dance all year long at the hotel until it burned to the ground 30 years later. The hotel was rebuilt but consumed by fire again in 1897. In those early days of settlement, wolves were often seen in the woods near the lake. Bears and cougars continued to be a common sight on the Saanich Peninsula as late as 1908.

The name of Swan Lake may commemorate James Swan, an American resident of Washington and self-taught ethnologist who visited Victoria in 1852.

Did you know?

The southern slope of Christmas Hill (once known as Lake Hill) was originally chosen by the Chinese Consolidated Benevolent Association for use as a cemetery for the location's Feng Shui, as it is flanked by two ridges, the lake, and two creeks. The oval shape of the lake at the time was thought to resemble a luminous pearl.

Despite land purchase records and verbal accounts, it appears that the area was never actually used as a cemetery. A different site was chosen after residents of the area at the time protested.

Birds love lakes...
but don't feed them bread!

Lakes and wetlands are popular places for many types of birds, particularly during migration periods. Spend a day in a secluded place along the shore and you are bound to see plenty of waterfowl, songbirds, and maybe even a few raptors such as owls, eagles, or osprey.

Spring is a good time to watch and listen for birds, as it is mating season. The courtship of mallard ducks is a spectacle to behold, often with several males pursuing a single female. After the spring mating season eggs start hatching and things get a bit quieter, as birds focus on protecting their offspring from predators.

Even birds that aren't water birds enjoy lakes. Swallows don't eat fish, but they are often seen darting over a lake's surface, performing fancy acrobatics as they hunt for insects.

Bread is not good for birds, as it contains sugars and chemicals that are unnatural to their diet. Bread has low nutritional value, can block a bird's digestive tract, and gives them the false feeling they are full. Wildlife should never rely on humans for food. If you still want to feed birds at a lake, give them whole grains such as flattened or rolled oats.

Blenkinsop Lake.
PHOTO BY ERNIE DICKEY

Blenkinsop Lake

Once known as Lost Lake, Blenkinsop Lake is a great rest stop and viewpoint for cyclists and walkers making their way along the Lochside Regional Trail, which stretches from Swartz Bay to Victoria and originally served as a railway. Another series of trails are close by, at Mount Douglas Park to the northwest. Accessible parking and bike racks are available on Lochside Drive, about 250 m south of the lake.

A trestle crosses over Blenkinsop Lake, offering views of the surrounding marshy wetlands, a much-needed habitat for birds of the region. This area has long been of keen interest for birdwatchers. Cooper's hawks and downy woodpeckers are residents, while migrant species such as swallows, warblers, or black-headed grosbeaks have been observed in April and May. Given the marshy shoreline, there is no real access to the water for swimming or paddling at Blenkinsop Lake.

The trestle was completed in 2000 and is built over top of the remnants of the original trestle bridge constructed in 1915 (during the First World War) by the Canadian Northern Pacific Railway.

Blenkinsop Lake was named after George Blenkinsop, born in Cornwall, England, in 1822. He joined the Hudson's Bay Company in 1840 as an apprentice to the sea service, and after serving in various posts for the company was eventually promoted to the rank of chief trader in charge of Fort Colville in 1857. He was later appointed as Indian Agent on the west coast of Vancouver Island in 1881.

Blenkinsop Lake is part of the Colquitz River watershed. Lochside Creek, Beckwith Creek, and Grosbeak Creek all flow into Blenkinsop Lake. Blenkinsop Creek is the outflow on the southeast end of the lake, and it flows southwards to Swan Lake, collecting waters from Cumberland Brook and Big Barn Creek on the way.

The trail at Fork Lake.
PHOTO BY ADAM UNGSTAD

Highlands

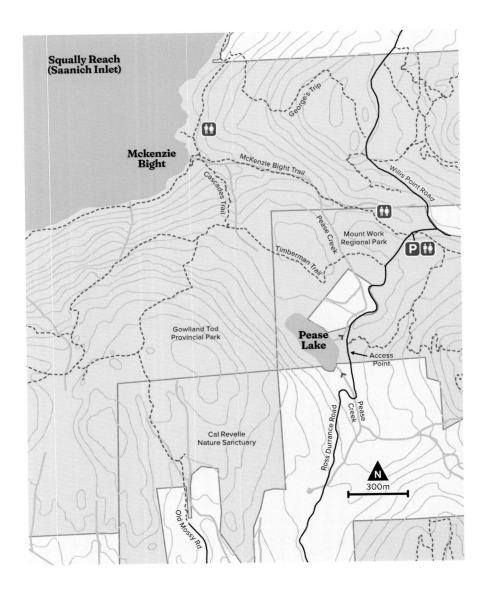

Squally Reach
(Saanich Inlet)

George's Trip

Mckenzie
Bight

McKenzie Bight Trail

Willis Point Road

Cascades Trail

Pease Creek

Mount Work
Regional Park

Timberman Trail

Gowlland Tod
Provincial Park

Pease
Lake

Access
Point

Pease
Creek

Cal Revelle
Nature Sanctuary

Ross Durrance Road

N
300m

Old Mossy Rd.

Pease Lake

Watershed: Pease Creek

Perimeter: 0.8 km

Elevation: 139 m

Max Depth: 6.0 m

Surface: 3.9 ha

Access: Mount Work Regional Park (Ross Durrance Road)

Surrounded by Douglas fir and cedar trees, Pease Lake is a quiet, little-known beauty found in the District of Highlands, in the fringes of Mount Work Regional Park. While most of Pease Lake is within park boundaries, the lake has been left largely undeveloped – indeed, there are no facilities, or even parking, at the single public access point.

Located on the southeast corner of the lake, the access point doesn't get much sun, so it's best to count on being on or in the water for this one. Bring a float-tube if you are fishing or an air mattress if you are swimming.

While you are there, listen for Pacific chorus frogs, also known as Pacific treefrogs. These indigenous frogs are loud considering their small size of 2–5 centimetres. In recent years the invasive American bullfrog has posed a significant threat to Pacific chorus frogs and many other species in the highlands.

Beaches & Swimming

The water is warm and there is easy entry to the lake, but there is no sand beach or wharf, and the access point is shaded by forest. The lack of a beach or facilities can make Pease Lake a peaceful place however, so bring something inflatable to float on if you'd like to soak up sun while you're there.

Hikes & Walks

There are no lakeside trails at Pease Lake, but there are plenty of great hiking trails in the nearby Gowlland Tod Provincial Park and Mount Work Regional Park. An enjoyable day hike is to visit the Saanich Inlet via the McKenzie Bight Trail. Make it a loop by returning via the

Pease Lake.
PHOTO BY ADAM UNGSTAD

Cascades Trail and the Timberman Trail. Budget at least two hours for the loop, and note that while the trail is well maintained there is a fair amount of steep declines and stairs on the way. In the wet season, watch for a pretty waterfall on the Cascades Trail.

Fishing

This lake is best suited for float tubes. There is minimal shoreline fishing as most of the lake is bordered by trees or private land. Unlike its neighbour, Durrance Lake, Pease Lake has not been regularly stocked with rainbow trout.

Paddling & Boats

Only carry-in boats are permitted on Pease Lake. Launching one will require some effort as the nearest parking is a ways away. Consider something inflatable – but use your lungs to fill it rather than a noisy motorized pump!

Cycling

A delightful route for experienced road cyclists is to arrive via the shady, hilly, narrow and winding Ross Durrance Road. After a good swim, return via Willis Point Road and the Interurban Trail.

Accessibility

The nearest accessible parking and washrooms are at Durrance Lake, which is too far to make Pease Lake particularly accessible. The short trail from the road to the lake is earthen and uneven – strollers will be ok, but Pease Lake is not well-suited for wheelchairs.

Parking, Washrooms, and Dogs

There is no parking at the Pease Lake access point – parking is found further north along Ross Durrance Road. Toilets are available at the parking lot, as well as along the McKenzie Bight Trail. Dogs are not allowed on beaches or picnic areas between June 1 and September 15, except to pass through on a leash.

Creeks & Watershed

Pease Lake has its own watershed, meaning it is not connected to other lakes in the area by streams or creeks. Pease Creek flows into Pease Lake at the southern end, and then carries water into the Saanich Inlet's McKenzie Bight. The McKenzie Bight Trail follows the northern portion of Pease Creek, and ends where the creek meets the ocean.

Local History

Pease Lake takes its name from early settlers Algernon (Algy) Henry Pease and his wife, Letty. They once had a residence on Elk Lake and owned land around McKenzie Bay before it became part of Gowlland Tod Provincial Park. Their daughter Rosalind has written about selling pinball machines up island and homemade plum wine during the time of prohibition. Before acquiring its current name, Pease Lake was known as Fourth Lake.

Early residents of Pease Lake were the Ross family. The son of immigrants from Scotland, Duncan Ross moved from Ontario to the Victoria area in 1890 and subsequently bought 160 acres of land around Pease Lake.

Mr. Ross left Victoria shortly afterwards to start a newspaper in the interior of BC. There he married his wife, Birdie Thomson, and together they moved to Ottawa after he was elected as a member of parliament. Following several other pursuits, the Ross family returned to Victoria in 1910 to build a home on Rockland Avenue.

Ross Durrance Road in the early 1910s.
PHOTO BY ROSS/ROBBINS FAMILY

By 1913 the family had built several extensions to the original log cabin at Pease Lake and proceeded to open Ross Ranch. At the time the only route to the ranch was a dirt road leading from Langford, which ended at their front door.

Pacific chorus frogs

Pacific chorus frogs, also known as Pacific treefrogs or *Pseudacris regilla*, are indigenous to Vancouver Island and make their home in riparian habitat. They are easy to identify, with a dark stripe across their eyes and toe pads to help their grip. Frogs are amphibians, meaning they are born in water but move to land. Through metamorphosis, tadpoles shift from breathing with gills in water like fish to breathing with lungs in air like mammals.

You'll hear the mating call of Pacific chorus frogs on warm, humid nights. Their songs are often used as ambient nature sounds in Hollywood movies, many of which are set in places where these frogs do not actually live. Aside from attracting a mate, these calls also help to space these frogs out, marking their territory.

Pacific chorus frogs can breed in ephemeral (temporary or seasonal) wetlands – a small advantage over the invasive, larger, and highly aggressive American bullfrog, which preys on them but thrives in perpetual (permanent) wetlands.

Coastal Indigenous peoples once believed that there is a Pacific chorus frog for every human on earth.

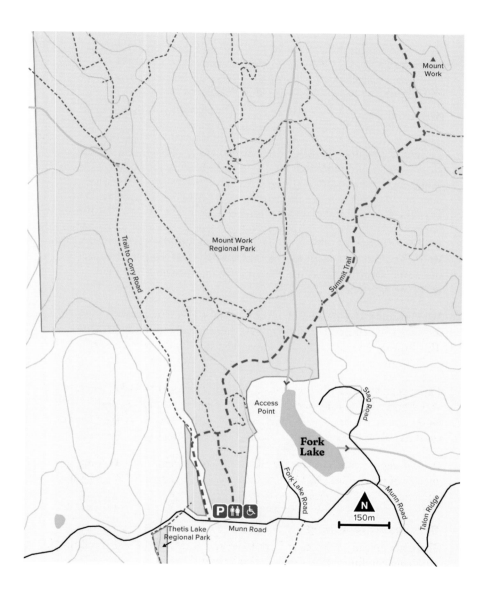

Fork Lake

Watershed: Craigflower Creek

Perimeter: 0.8 km

Elevation: 216 m

Max Depth: 10 m

Surface: 3.1 ha

Access: via Mount Work Regional Park (Munn Road)

Known as a habitat for owls, eagles, frogs, newts, deer, woodpeckers, and many other locals, Fork Lake is the perfect place for people of all ages and abilities to connect with the natural world.

The lake is mostly surrounded by private land and residences, but the northwest corner borders Mount Work Regional Park and serves as the trailhead for the Summit Trail, which leads to the summit of Mount Work. You can catch a glimpse of the lake while in the park, but access to the water is quite limited and requires wading through thick bushes and shoreline vegetation.

While you are there, don't miss the magical 630-metre accessible loop trail, which leads through tall evergreens and rich undergrowth. This little-known loop is an absolute delight for walkers of all ages and abilities.

Pay special attention to the ground on your visit to Fork Lake, where you'll find a fascinating variety of mushrooms, ferns, mosses, and woodland flowers on the forest floor. Stay on the trails (and keep your dog on the trails too) so you don't disturb these delicate locals.

A 2006 report published by the BC Lake Stewardship Society found two species of pond lilies (*Nuphar*), two species of pond weeds (*Potamogeton*), and coontail (*Ceratophyllum*) in Fork Lake.

Beaches & Swimming

There are no sand beaches at Fork Lake and access to the water is limited, requiring careful footing through shrubs and shoreline vegetation.

A partial view of Fork Lake.
PHOTO BY ADAM UNGSTAD

Hikes & Walks

A 630 m accessible walking loop is a delight for all to connect with
the forest, but requires a detour to see a view of the lake. The trail
is smooth gravel, with gradual slopes that lead through a medley of
evergreens and rich understory of indigenous shrubs, ferns, mosses,
and woodland flowers.

For hikers, the 11 km moderate-to-challenging Summit Trail leads
from the north end of Fork Lake up to the summit of Mount Work,
and then down the other side to Ross Durrance Road, with swimming
opportunities at Durrance Lake a few minutes farther.

Another option for hikers is to cross to the southern side of Munn Road
and head towards Stewart Mountain via the northern tip of Thetis Lake
Regional Park.

Corry Road

At the northwest corner of the accessible loop trail you'll find a smaller,
single-track trail branching off. This trail itself is a largely unknown
historical feature: Corry Road.

Named after Frederick Charles Corry, Corry Road was built in the 1920s to connect families living at Fork Lake with their neighbours living near Third Lake, thereby providing a much easier route between what are now known as Munn Road and Ross Durrance Road.

This relatively easy trail falls mostly within Mount Work Regional Park, but parts of it do pass through private land. The largely undisturbed second-growth forest showcases the beauty of the natural world and is enjoyed for photography, bird-watching, and outdoor art. Along this trail you'll find a variety of indigenous trees, including Douglas fir, arbutus, and cedar.

Fishing

This lake is best suited for float tubes, as there is no shoreline fishing and no direct access to launch carry-in boats. Fork Lake has not been stocked with fish since the early 1990s, but there may still be natural populations of trout.

Paddling & Boats

Access for carry-in boats is limited and requires navigating bushes and shoreline vegetation. While canoes or kayaks are not recommended, the undisturbed shoreline on the west side of Fork Lake would be an interesting place to explore with a stand-up paddle board.

Cycling

Biking to Fork Lake will require some riding on roads. Using the Galloping Goose Regional Trail, take Burnside Road West to Prospect Lake Road, and from there, branch off to Munn Road.

If you're up for a workout and have plenty of time left after your visit to Fork Lake, continue on Munn Road and turn right onto Millstream Lake Road, which leads through the hilly District of Highlands, a world away from the urban streets of Victoria.

Accessibility

A fully accessible 630 m loop trail starts at the Munn Road parking lot and leads through ferns, shrubs, mosses, and wild woodland flowers. The accessible loop does not offer views of Fork Lake itself, but is still a fantastic place to take in the natural world of the Pacific northwest. The trail has a smooth gravel surface and some gradual slopes.

Parking, Washrooms, and Dogs

Three designated accessible parking stalls and accessible pit toilets are available at the Munn Road parking lot. Dogs must be under control and on trails.

Creeks & Watershed

Fork Lake is part of the Craigflower Creek Watershed. Water from Fork Lake flows eastward, joins Craigflower Creek via a smaller creek, and then passes through Pike Lake before making its way to Portage Inlet.

Local History

Close to Fork Lake, but not within park boundaries, is the Fork Lake Ditch. It was built in the early 1900s and is considered a symbol of the pioneer drive to not only survive, but to move beyond subsistence.

The ditch was dug and blasted by a team led by Frank Gregory, an early property owner. Gregory had decided that by lowering the level of the water at Fork Lake he would be able to create more land for grazing for his livestock – and he was right.

The ditch allowed water from Fork Lake to drain into Fizzle Lake (on the south side of Munn Road) and reduced the depth of Fork Lake by nearly three meters, thereby providing 1.7 acres of new land for his livestock. Knowledge of this impressive feat leaves one to wonder about the original shape and size of Fork Lake.

SKATYNG. — Gregory's + Bernards

The Bernard and Gregory families skating on Fork Lake in winter of 1911.
PHOTO BY JESSIE BERNARD

Western skunk cabbage

Western skunk cabbage (*Lysichiton americanus*), also known as swamp lantern or Skeena lily, is a familiar sight along Victoria's bogs, creeks, and lakeshores. Its bright, canary-yellow blooms make it easy to spot. A hiker's nose can detect it by the skunky smell it emits. The strong odour attracts pollinating insects including flies, midges, and beetles.

These plants are part of the *Araceae* family. The central, club-like spike inside the flower of a skunk cabbage is called a spadix, and the leaf-like bract that cups the spadix is called a spathe.

British Columbia Indigenous peoples used skunk cabbage leaves to wrap food (similar to how we use wax paper today) and to keep foods like meat, fish, and vegetables separate while steaming them.

Where is Millstream Lake?

Millstream Lake Road leads into the District of Highlands, which seems to indicate there is a Millstream Lake somewhere close by. Yet try looking for Millstream Lake on a map, and you won't find it. So why is there a road named after a lake that doesn't exist?

Most lakes have been known by different names throughout the thousands of years they've been around, so it's possible that one of the lakes in the District of Highlands used to be known by this name. However there are no official records of this.

One theory is that the road was meant to be called Millstream Lakes Road, referring to a number of lakes rather than just one. Watch the signs with road names carefully in the District of Highlands and you'll find other oddities, such as the intersection of Munn Road and Munn's Road.

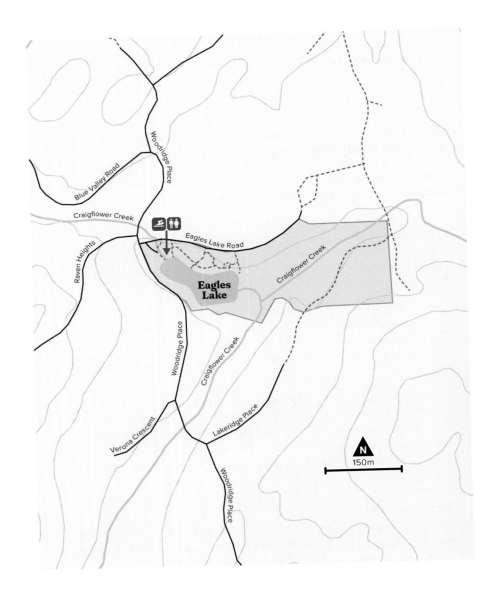

Eagles Lake

Watershed: Craigflower Creek   **Surface:** 1 ha

Elevation: 22 m   **Access:** Eagles Lake Municipal Park
(Eagles Lake Road)

Eagles Lake is a small, hidden swimming hole. If you didn't know better, you'd expect to find a rope swing with a tire at the end hanging over the water. The lake is surrounded by cedar with an undergrowth of salal and Himalayan blackberries, providing habitat for wildlife such as the great-horned owl, Steller's jay, black tailed deer, and American mink.

Eagles Lake Park is one of only two municipal parks in the District of Highlands and is a fantastic place to spend an afternoon with the kids, although parking is limited. The eastern side of the park borders a BC Hydro right-of-way, which is often used to access Mount Work Regional Park.

One of the park's unique features is a composting toilet that was built by volunteers of the Highlands Parks and Recreation Association and Eco-Sense. This luxury outhouse features walls made of clay, sand, and straw; a living roof; and even a time capsule within its walls. It was built to last for 500 years.

Eagles Lake itself is unique among its peers as it is young compared to other lakes nearby. While most lakes in the highlands were created by pioneers through the construction of dams in the late 1800s or early 1900s, Eagles Lake was created in 1976 through the removal of a spring-fed wetland – much of which can still be seen beyond the lake on the east side of the park.

Beaches & Swimming
This lake has a small sand beach and warm water – best for families rather than sun seekers. This is a small, shallow lake, so expect more of a doggie paddle than a proper swim. Other than the beach, most of the shoreline is marshy, so consider bringing something to float on.

Eagles Lake in the District of Highlands.
PHOTO BY ADAM UNGSTAD

Hikes & Walks

A trail at the end of Eagles Lake Road leads to a BC Hydro right-of-way. Heading north on the right-of-way eventually leads to Mount Work Regional Park, with a connection to Killarney Lake.

Fishing

Fishing is not permitted from the shore at Eagles Lake. There are no records to show that this small lake has been stocked, likely due to its small size.

Paddling & Boats

There is easy access for carry-in boats or stand-up paddle boards.

Cycling

Cycling to Eagles Lake will require riding along some busy roads with narrow shoulders. Exit the Galloping Goose Regional Trail at Burnside Road West, turn onto Prospect Lake Road, then follow Munn Road until you reach Woodridge Place, which leads to Eagles Lake Road.

Accessibility

The trail from Eagles Lake Road to the beach is less than 50 m and easy for strollers, however the surface is earthen and may be a challenge for wheelchairs. There is no accessible parking.

Parking, Washrooms, and Dogs

There is no parking lot at Eagles Lake. Respect those that live there and follow signage. A unique, compostable toilet is found at the main beach. Dogs must be on a leash in the park and are not allowed on the beach.

Creeks & Watershed

Water enters Eagles Lake via a creek labelled on some sources as Munn Creek and others as Craigflower Creek, as well as groundwater. The lake's primary outflow is Craigflower Creek on the eastern side, which passes through Pike Lake before draining into Portage Inlet (the northern end of the Gorge Waterway).

Local History

Eagles Lake was not named after the birds circling above, as one might expect. The lake was actually named after civil servant Frank Eagles, who served in the 1960s. Eagles are present in the area however, so you may see one while visiting!

Mary Lake
(Restricted access)

Mary Lake is surrounded by the Mary Lake Nature Sanctuary, which is dedicated to conservation of the natural environment. Much of the area is riparian (stream side and wetland), with seven ecosystems including examples of the rare coastal Douglas fir forest and five different endangered plant communities.

Mary Lake and the varied habitats of the sanctuary provide home for amphibians, bats, owls, and waterfowl such as mergansers and bufflehead. Beaver and river otters can be seen swimming along the shoreline on occasion. The property acts as an important wildlife corridor between Thetis Lake Regional Park and Gowlland Tod Provincial Park.

Swimming is prohibited in Mary Lake because it is shallow and sensitive to pollution. Earsman Creek flows through the lake during winter months and is dry during the summer and early fall. Dogs and other domestic animals are not allowed on the property. In keeping with the conservation values, the Mary Lake Nature Sanctuary welcomes visitors on the second Sunday of each month or by request for guided tours and special events. Forest bathing, also called nature therapy or ecotherapy, is promoted to encourage a deeper connection to nature.

Trails are mostly level and considered easy. A paved driveway allows people who use walkers or wheelchairs to get into the heart of nature. The Earsman Creek and East Loop trails show off the lake, streams, skunk cabbage wetlands, sword fern, alder woodlands, and other natural features.

Local History
Victoria artist Gertrude Snider initiated conservation after the degrading effects of earlier use of the area. Conservation was also foremost in mind when Peter and Hazel Brotherston bought the property from her in 1963.

Mergansers on Mary Lake.
PHOTO BY MARY LAKE NATURE SANCTUARY

The property was purchased in 2016 by the Greater Victoria Greenbelt Society with a mortgage provided by Vancity. The last of the mortgage was paid off by a grant from the Province of BC in 2019. Protection and restoration of the natural ecosystems continue to be the main focus at this unique property.

The Greater Victoria Greenbelt Society has partnered with the Tsartlip First Nation so that both western science and Indigenous wisdom and culture can guide the sanctuary's future.

Are pondweeds actually weeds?

Pondweeds are a genus, or a large group, of aquatic plants known technically as *Potamogeton,* derived from the Greek *potamos* (river) and *geiton* (neighbour).

There are many species of *Potamogeton* found in Victoria's lakes, both indigenous and non-indigenous. Given that aquatic plants like pondweeds provide the basis of life in ponds and lakes, perhaps we could have kept their original naming as 'pond neighbours'.

Many invasive and aggressive submersed plants found in places like Elk/Beaver Lake and Shawnigan Lake, such as *Myriophyllum spicatum* (Eurasian water-milfoil), are not part of the *Potamogeton* genus.

Help make sure that aquatic plants don't move between lakes by draining, washing, and drying your boating equipment each time you leave a lake.

View Royal

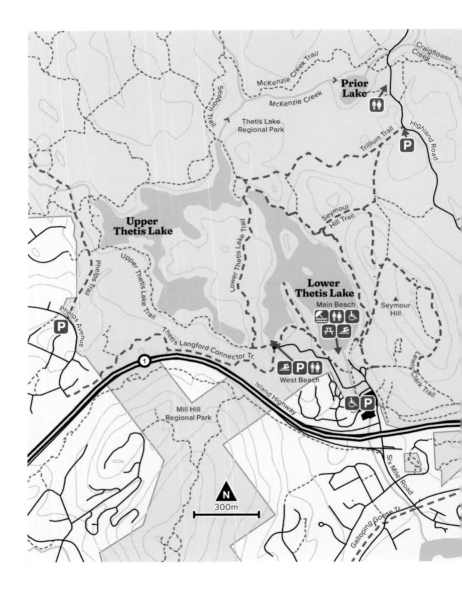

Thetis Lake

Watershed: Craigflower Creek

Elevation: 48 m

Surface: 67.8 ha

Perimeter: 4.8 km

Max Depth: 14 m

Access: Whitehead Park (Goward Road), Echo Place Boat Launch, South Prospect Lake Park (Prospect Lake Road), or Estelline Park (Estelline Road).

From secluded coves along the shoreline to clifftop views and magnificent surrounding forest, Thetis Lake has it all. It is an ideal place to paddle and a great destination for cyclists. Thetis Lake exemplifies the best of Victoria's lakes for lake enthusiasts of all types, with opportunities for swimming, sunbathing, hiking, and fishing.

The trails around the lake's beaches, cliffs, and secluded coves lead through Garry oak ecosystems and Douglas fir forests, providing a chance for all to connect with nature in its finest form. There are few, if any, cities in Canada with such easy access to a lake that has as much personality as Thetis Lake.

A short walk from the main parking lot at the end of Six Mile Road is the sandy Main Beach, which bustles in the summer. There are washrooms and changing facilities, picnic tables, a water fountain, and sometimes food vendors.

Often overlooked, the second parking lot on the southwest side of Lower Thetis has a smaller, shadier beach called the West Beach by the CRD and the Dog Beach by locals. This beach is ideal for launching small boats or letting dogs get into the water.

From an ecological perspective, Thetis Lake is surrounded by mid-growth hemlock, cedar, arbutus, and Douglas fir trees. In the springtime watch for wildflowers in the hills nearby, including shooting star, white fawn lily, and spring gold.

In the summertime dragonflies, damselflies, butterflies, moths, and caterpillars buzz, flutter, and crawl about. Thetis Lake is also home to many insects that go unseen – either too small to be seen with the naked eye or living under the water's surface. Watch for evidence of woodpeckers hunting for grubs and boring insects, as well as sap suckers in search of nectar. Moths and other insects are attracted to the sap, and in so doing become additional food for the birds.

At dusk watch for the bats that live in the hills nearby. They can be quite a sight as they socialize, swirl, and congregate around the lake. Deer, river otter, and even the occasional cougar have also been known to call Thetis Lake Regional Park home.

Beaches & Swimming

There are two sand beaches on the lower lake and many other secluded access points and rocky outcrops along the shoreline of both the upper and lower lakes.

Hikes & Walks

There are many trails in Thetis Lake Regional Park that offer different routes, views, landscapes, and ecosystems, making it perfect for hikers and walkers of all abilities and interests.

The 2.2 km loop around the lower lake is a decent stroll with good views recommended for a first visit. While the trail is wide and well-groomed, there is some change in elevation. The loop around the upper lake is more rustic, with a narrow, rockier trail. The trail around the upper lake is approximately 2.6 km and has a number of benches where one can pause for a break or a picnic. Watch the forest undergrowth for salal berries and plenty of ferns.

Those looking for an epic day hike can branch off the upper loop trail and head to the north end of the park via Scafe Hill and Stewart Mountain. Once you reach Munn Road, continue past Fork Lake to the summit of Mount Work and then to Ross Durrance Road. From there you can continue farther via Gowlland Tod Provincial Park to McKenzie Bight on the shore of Squally Reach (the Saanich Inlet).

Thetis Lake.
PHOTO BY MIKE MUNROE

Fishing

Thetis Lake is regularly stocked with rainbow trout. Coastal cutthroat trout, smallmouth bass, and even perch are also present. Given the unique shoreline, there are many places to explore and find a favourite spot to cast. Spring and fall are the best times for trout fishing, while the warmer months are best for bass.

Paddling & Boats

With secluded coves, cliffs, an island, and many other highlights, Thetis Lake is a delight to explore by paddling. The best place to launch a carry-in boat is from the West Beach. Boats with electric motors are permitted on Thetis Lake.

Cycling

Access the lake via the Galloping Goose Regional Trail and Six Mile Road, or the Thetis-Langford Connector Trail. Cycling is not permitted on the lakeshore trails, but there are routes for mountain bikers in the park – watch for signage. Bike racks are provided at the Main Beach and West Beach, as well as the intersection between the Lower Thetis Lake Trail and the Trillium Trail.

Accessibility

The loop around the lower lake is wide and well groomed, but has a number of points where the steep grade is not accessible for wheelchairs, and will be difficult for strollers. The loop around the upper lake is narrow and undulating, not recommended for anyone with limited mobility. A nearby, wheelchair accessible alternative is the Elsie King Trail at Francis/King Regional Park. Note however that this trail does not offer a view of the lake.

Parking, Washrooms and Dogs

The main parking lot is at the end of Six Mile Road, with further parking towards the West Beach. Both offer accessible parking stalls. Highland Road, Phelps Ave, and Munn Road also offer parking. Accessible toilets and a change room are available at the Main Beach, with additional toilets available at the West Beach. Dogs must be on a leash to pass through the Main Beach from June 1 – September 15 and must otherwise be under control and on trails. The trails around the shoreline of Upper and Lower Thetis Lake are popular with dog walkers year-round.

Creeks & Watershed

Thetis Lake is part of the Craigflower Creek watershed. Water from Thetis Lake passes through Prior Lake before joining Craigflower Creek, eventually emptying into Portage Inlet.

Local History

The woods near what is now known as Thetis Lake were long used by the Indigenous people to hunt deer, bear, and elk. They would also harvest clams from the inlet below and would steam, mash, cook, and roast the indigenous sprouts and berries found in the undergrowth for food.

Credit for the thriving ecosystem surrounding Thetis Lake is given in no small part to the Thetis Park Nature Sanctuary Association. The association was formed in 1957 and is the first formal nature sanctuary in Canada.

Thetis Lake was named after a ship in the British navy – the HMS Thetis. The ship was sent to protect British rights to gold found in Haida Gwaii (formerly the Queen Charlotte Islands) in 1852. Thetis Island and Thetis Cove were also named after this ship.

Doug Clement Photography © 2018

Thetis Lake.
PHOTO BY DOUG CLEMENT

Thetis Lake once played a supporting role in the City of Victoria's water supply. In 1864 the Spring Ridge Water Company laid log pipes to transport water from Elk Lake to the city, and Thetis Lake was then connected to the system in the 1870s as a reserve supply. This network was later replaced by water transported from Sooke Lake in the early 1900s.

Over the years the parkland at Thetis Lake has seen a patchwork of additions and extensions, with thanks to the efforts of the Capital Regional District and local conservation groups.

Did you know?

Although Thetis Lake was originally one lake, it was separated into two when a dike was installed to create access for a fire road. In later years, a culvert was installed under the dike to link the two lakes again, allowing paddlers to explore both lakes. As such there is some debate over whether this is one lake or two – the BC Geological Survey states that the official name of this waterbody is Thetis Lake, but that the feature type was changed from "lake" to "lakes" in 2003.

Francis/King Park

If the lake is a bit busy for you, take a detour to the nearby Francis/King Regional Park, where you'll find a 750-metre wheelchair-accessible trail leading through a forest with trees up to two meters thick, 75 meters high, and 500 years old. Watch for turkey vultures, hawks, woodpeckers, sapsuckers, hummingbirds, swallows, chickadees, and wrens. On the ground, look for snakes, frogs, and ants. Francis/King Regional Park is an exceptional place to take the family, young or old.

McKenzie Lake

For those who enjoy a good, brisk hike through wilderness trails, explore the rocky and sometimes narrow single-track trail to McKenzie Lake in Thetis Lake Regional Park. The McKenzie Creek Trail, which starts a bit farther up Highland Road from the trailhead to Prior Lake, leads through an impressive forest, wetlands, small plank bridges, and across log rounds.

While the southern tip of McKenzie Lake borders Thetis Lake Regional Park, most of the shoreline is surrounded by privately owned land. The southern tip has been left to grow as it chooses, so you'll need to navigate a fair amount of undergrowth to access the water.

McKenzie Lake has not been stocked with fish by the Freshwater Fisheries Society of BC, but there are small trout to be found in this lake. Bring a float tube, as casting from the shore will be difficult. There are no washrooms at McKenzie Lake.

McKenzie Lake is part of the Craigflower Creek watershed. Water enters McKenzie Lake via a creek that starts at Teanook Lake. McKenzie Creek is the primary outflow of McKenzie Lake, and water then passes through Prior Lake before joining Craigflower Creek and emptying into Portage Inlet.

Hooded Mergansers

Victoria is a favourite winter destination for a species of smaller ducks called *Lophodytes cucullatus* (commonly, hooded mergansers). It is common to see these ducks at Thetis Lake between August to April.

Mergansers are known as "fish ducks" because they dive underwater to hunt for crayfish and small fish, as well as small frogs, newts, tadpoles, and aquatic insects. They are also known to fly very fast for ducks.

As with many birds, hooded mergansers are masters of deception. If you see a female acting as if she has a broken wing, it may be making a show to lure predators (or you) to her and away from her young.

Prior Lake

Watershed: Craigflower Creek

Perimeter: 0.4 km

Elevation: 40 m

Max Depth: 5 m

Surface: 1.1 ha

Access: Thetis Lake Regional Park (Highland Rd)

Prior Lake is a tiny paradise that has been used by naturists for as long as anyone can remember. A naturist, not to be confused with a naturalist, is a person who seeks to enjoy nature in a completely natural state – that is, without clothing. The lake's natural beauty, small size, warm water, and ease of access make it a fantastic place to swim or sunbathe.

The philosophy of naturism includes being considerate to others, and on your first visit to Prior Lake you will find naturists to be friendly and respectful – to you and the natural environment around them. Prior Lake generally has a more laid-back, mature feel to it than its noisier neighbour. If you are hesitating on your visit to Prior Lake because you are not sure what to expect, take the plunge. You will be glad you did!

Beaches & Swimming

There is a small beach and a dock that goes out into the lake. If you go on a hot summer afternoon, you'll find plenty of sunbathers on the dock – but there's always room for more. The dock generally keeps all lake-goers in close proximity, so expect some social activity while you are there. Bring an air mattress or a tube to float on if you'd prefer a little more space to yourself.

To really know Prior Lake, you need to go there just before dusk on a late summer's evening. Enjoy the silhouettes of the trees around you while you swim through the silky water and listen to the serenade of the Pacific tree frogs who call the lake home.

Prior Lake on a warm afternoon in late May.
PHOTO BY PRIOR LAKE NATURIST PRESERVATION COMMITTEE

Hikes & Walks

There are no trails around Prior Lake, but access to the McKenzie Creek trail is a bit farther north on Highland Road. Thetis Lake Regional Park offers many other hiking and walking trails to explore.

Fishing

The lake is stocked regularly with rainbow trout. Coastal cutthroat trout, smallmouth bass, and sunfish have also been found here. There is a dock to cast from, but it will be crowded in warmer months, so a float-tube or carry-in boat will be useful. As usual, bass will be close to the vegetation along the marshy shore.

Paddling & Boats

No motorized boats are permitted at Prior Lake. Those with carry-in boats such as canoes or kayaks will likely be more interested in larger lakes, but the marshy shoreline of Prior Lake is an ideal place to explore with a stand-up paddleboard.

Cycling

Prior Lake is a great alternative to Thetis Lake for cyclists looking for a good bike ride and a swim. It is a fairly steep incline to get there, but remember that you'll get to ride down the same hill after a refreshing swim!

Exit the Galloping Goose Regional Trail at Burnside Road West, turn left on Watkiss Way and follow Highland Road to the lake. Cycling is not permitted on the trail to the lake.

Accessibility

The short 200 m gravel trail descending to the beach is a bit steep at points and is generally not considered wheelchair accessible, but it has been done before. Strollers and canes will be fine. There are no accessible washrooms or accessible parking stalls.

Parking, Washrooms, and Dogs

Parking is available on Highland Road, and there are seasonal toilets at the lake. Dogs are not permitted on the dock or at the main beach from June 1 – September 15.

Creeks & Watershed

Prior Lake is part of the Craigflower Creek Watershed. Waters from Upper Thetis Lake and Lower Thetis Lake pass through Prior Lake, as do waters from Teanook Lake and McKenzie Lake. The main outflow of Prior Lake takes water on to Craigflower Creek, which eventually empties into Portage Inlet (the north end of the Gorge Waterway).

Local History

There have been three docks at Prior Lake through the years. The first one was small and known to sink below the waterline when it got crowded. The second, much larger dock was provided by the City of Victoria, but then subsequently removed when Thetis Lake Park was transferred to the Capital Regional District (CRD) in 1993.

The naturists who had been enjoying the dock for decades mobilized to raise funds towards the construction of a new dock, for which the CRD provided the remainder of financing and constructed in 1994.

Prior Lake was originally known as Little Thetis Lake and acquired its current name in 1934 after Lieutenant-Colonel The Honorable Edward Gawlor Prior, a man whose history is deeply interwoven with the development of Victoria.

Mr. Prior arrived on Vancouver Island in 1873 and was originally employed as a mining engineer. In 1878 he owned a hardware store in a building that still stands at the corner of Government and Johnson Streets in downtown Victoria. Mr. Prior later moved into politics, being elected to the provincial legislature in the late 1880s and 1890s, eventually serving as the premier of British Columbia from 1902–1903. Long known as a hard worker, Mr. Prior died in 1920 while serving as lieutenant governor.

American bullfrog: an invasive threat

Lithobates catesbeianus, commonly known as American bullfrog, is a highly aggressive, territorial carnivore that is threatening indigenous species in lakes near Victoria and across Vancouver Island.

One of the world's most invasive species, the American bullfrog weighs up to 1.5 pounds and eats anything it can fit in its mouth, including indigenous Pacific chorus frogs, salamanders, snakes, and even ducklings. If American bullfrogs don't directly eat other animals at our lakes, they compete against them for food, often leaving little left.

A single female American bullfrog can lay 20,000 eggs, and a good number of these will survive, given that other animals don't generally have a taste for them. Preventing the proliferation of these predators is an uphill battle and we need all hands on deck. To learn more about how you can help, contact the Invasive Species Council of BC.

Lakes: nature's archivists

Understanding the past can be key to predicting the future.

The rings in a log of a tree can tell about what happened during a tree's lifespan, but most trees don't live longer than a few hundred years. The glacier-formed lakes on Vancouver Island are thousands of years old however, and unlike a tree, a lake can document trends and events over very long periods of time.

The bottom of a lake collects anything that falls below the lake's surface, including sediments and particles from the water or the air above, and dead matter from plants or animals. As centuries pass, layers of mud build on top of each other, and create a historical timeline. The science of studying sediment profiles below a lake's floor is called paleoliminology.

Sediments from the bottom of Elk/Beaver Lake, Prospect Lake and Langford Lake have been collected and analysed by researchers, who use things like fossilized pollen grains and charcoal fragments to understand changes in vegetation and fire disturbance over time.

The paleoliminology research done on local lakes indicates that the early Holocene period (11,700 to 7000 years ago) was warmer and drier on Vancouver Island than it is now, giving insight to how our climate may change in the future.

Langford

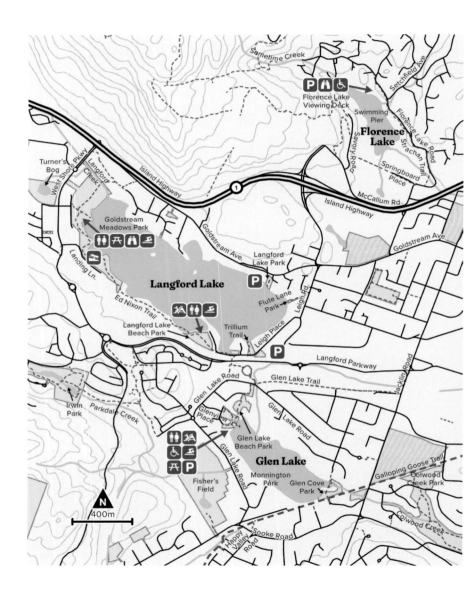

Langford Lake

Watershed: Goldstream River

Elevation: 67 m

Surface: 59.2 ha

Perimeter: 4.7 km

Max Depth: 17 m

Access: Langford Lake Beach Park (Leigh Place), Goldstream Meadows Park (Landing Lane), or Langford Lake Park (Shelby Place)

At 61 hectares in size, Langford Lake is one of the larger lakes in the Victoria area. It has many facilities and a variety of access points for great swimming and fishing opportunities. A boat launch on Landing Lane ensures access for kayaks, canoes, and boats with electric motors.

The main beach is a delight for families and the Ed Nixon Trail offers a boardwalk for a chance to get above the water, with options to connect to other municipal trails further along. The north and east sides of Langford Lake are largely taken up by residences, but there are a few pocket parks that provide additional access to the water, some of which have limited parking and can be used to launch a carry-in boat.

Langford Lake is a favourite for fishing, offering good sized rainbow trout, cutthroat trout, and smallmouth bass. If you don't have a boat, there is a small fishing dock found along the Ed Nixon Trail, about 300 meters south of the boat launch.

Beaches & Swimming

The main beach, with washrooms and an accessible playground, is found at Langford Lake Beach Park, off the end of Leigh Place. This is a popular spot, and rightfully so! With plenty of sun, picnic tables, and a floating platform to swim to, this beach is ideal for the entire family.

Langford Lake Park and Goldstream Meadows Park are great alternatives for swimmers who aren't interested in playgrounds, and there are a few shaded access points along the Ed Nixon Trail.

An arbutus tree at Langford Lake.
PHOTO BY MURRAY SHARRATT

Hikes & Walks

Starting from Langford Lake Beach Park, the Ed Nixon Trail leads west via a boardwalk with enjoyable views, and then through peaceful parkland of Douglas fir trees and dull Oregon grape in the undergrowth. The trail follows the southwestern curve of the lake, eventually leading to a boardwalk over the marshes of Goldstream Meadows Park. It is likely that the southern side of the lake has remained undeveloped due to the Esquimalt & Nanaimo Railway, which used to run parallel to where parts of the Ed Nixon Trail is now.

Fishing

Stocked regularly with rainbow trout (Fraser Valley and Blackwater River strains). Coastal cutthroat trout yearlings were released in 2019. Non-indigenous species of fish are present as well, including smallmouth bass, brown catfish, pumpkinseed sunfish, and yellow perch.

There are plenty of opportunities to fish from the shore along the Ed Nixon trail, including a raised boardwalk and a fishing pier. On the water, watch for the aerator, which improves the quality of water in the lake and attracts small trout – this is a good place to troll. Bigger trout and bass will be along the smaller bays, islands, and near vegetation. Chironomids and baitfish work well for bass here.

Paddling & Boats

Given its size, Langford Lake is an ideal place to explore by boat. For craft that need to be launched with a trailer, a boat launch is found on the west end of the lake, off Landing Lane. Boats with electric motors are permitted. Langford Lake Park and Flute Lane Park can also be used to launch carry-in boats.

Cycling

The best route to get to Langford Lake is to exit the Galloping Goose Regional Trail at Glen Lake Road, and then head north along the residential roads until you reach the Langford Parkway. When the E&N Rail Trail is complete it will provide a more direct connection between the Galloping Goose Regional Trail and Langford Lake.

Accessibility

The Ed Nixon Trail is well-groomed, wide, and considered easy but not wheelchair accessible due to some inclines. Langford Lake Beach Park has easy access to the water, an enjoyable boardwalk, accessible washrooms, and an accessible playground. The trails at Goldstream Meadows Park are level and considered easy, however do not offer many views of the lake – the boat launch is a good place to start if you are exploring this area.

Parking, Washrooms, and Dogs

The main parking is close to Langford Beach Park, with several options along Langford Parkway. Langford Lake Beach Park has permanent accessible washrooms, and seasonal toilets can usually be found at the boat launch. Different parks and access points have different rules for dogs, so watch for signage.

Creeks & Watershed

While it seems difficult to separate Langford Lake from its neighbours – Glen Lake and Florence Lake – the three are actually in separate watersheds. Before the construction of the Esquimalt and Nanaimo (E&N) railway in the 1880s, water from Langford Lake moved to Glen Lake and then continued southwards. Today, however, water from Langford Lake empties into Finlayson Arm to the north. Langford Lake is part of the Goldstream River watershed.

Local History

Langford Lake takes its name from Captain Edward Langford, who arrived in Victoria in 1851. He was tasked with managing a 200-acre farm for a subsidiary of the Hudson's Bay Company and was known for welcoming visitors as a means of finding potential suitors for his five daughters.

The construction of the E&N railway in the 1880s drove many more visitors to the Langford area. Many passengers would never have known about Langford Lake, however, as it was hidden from view behind dense forest.

Osprey

From spring to autumn, watch for large brown and white raptors commonly known as osprey hunting for fish near Langford's lakes. The scientific name for these impressive birds of prey is *Pandion haliaetus*.

Osprey feed almost entirely on fish, so naturally they love lakes. While ospreys and eagles both have four talons (claws) on each leg, ospreys can swivel one of theirs from front to back – a handy feature if you are carrying a slippery, wriggly fish while flying through the air! Bald eagles have been known to steal fish from ospreys rather than hunt for their own meal.

What are raptors?

Raptors are birds of prey, meaning they feed on animal flesh. They are known to have hooked bills and sharp talons. Eagles, osprey, hawks, and owls are raptors you may see near the lakes and wetlands of Victoria.

The Cy Jenkins boardwalk at Glen Lake.
PHOTO BY ADAM UNGSTAD

Glen Lake

Watershed: Colwood Creek

Elevation: 67 m

Surface: 16.6 ha

Perimeter: 2.0 km

Max Depth: 14 m

Access: Glen Lake Beach Park (Shoreview Drive) or Glen Cove Park (Galloping Goose Regional Trail)

An urban haven, Glen Lake has a sunny beach, an accessible playground, several piers, a floating boardwalk, and even a space set aside for dogs to enjoy the water.

The main attraction is Glen Lake Beach Park, which has everything you need to enjoy an afternoon with the whole family. Private residences border much of the lake but there are several other access points, each with their own unique character and setting. Cyclists using the Galloping Goose Regional Trail will pass by a second pier on the lake's southeast corner. The forested Glen Cove Park offers a floating boardwalk along the Cy Jenkins Trail, and the much smaller and largely unknown Monnington Park offers a small wooden dock.

In the right season, bird watchers can expect to see chipping sparrows, hairy woodpeckers, belted kingfishers, northern flickers, and rufous hummingbirds at Glen Lake.

Beaches & Swimming

Glen Lake is a great place for swimming. The best access points are at Glen Lake Beach Park, and alternatively, the pier found off the Galloping Goose Trail.

At the main beach you will find a fully accessible playground, spray park, outdoor shower, picnic areas, washrooms, plenty of open green space, and a fishing pier, not to mention a separate beach set aside just for the furry family members. The fishing pier has been a longstanding feature and provides a chance to get out on the water without getting wet.

PHOTO BY ADAM UNGSTAD

Hikes & Walks

The Cy Jenkins Trail in Glen Cove Park will be of most interest to walkers. The 200 m trail features a unique floating boardwalk with some seating, so pause to admire the aquatic vegetation and marshlands. As the seasons change, watch for butterflies, shorebirds, herons, otters, and other resident or migrating creatures.

The short Glen Lake Trail is useful to connect to other trails nearby. It leads north from the main beach and can be used as part of a route to the nearby Langford Lake Beach Park, and from there, the Ed Nixon Trail. Watch for Douglas fir, cedars, salal, ferns, and blackberry bushes. Another place to explore near Glen Lake is the wetlands of Fisher's Field, on the south side of Glen Lake Road.

Fishing

Glen Lake has been stocked with fish since the 1920s. The lake is generally stocked with rainbow trout each spring and fall. Coastal cutthroat trout, brown catfish, pumpkinseed sunfish, and smallmouth bass are also present. There are several piers to cast from, and the southern end of the lake has more riparian vegetation.

Paddling & Boats
Carry-in boats can be launched with ease from Glen Lake Beach Park. In general, paddlers will likely be most interested in the south end of the lake.

Cycling
The pier directly off the Galloping Goose Regional Trail is a perfect destination or rest stop for cyclists. Enjoy!

Accessibility
Glen Lake Beach Park is one of the most accessible lakeshore parks in the Victoria area, with accessible parking, washrooms, beach, playground, and a fishing/viewing dock. Glen Cove Park on the eastern side of the lake is not wheelchair accessible but can be done with a stroller.

Parking, Washrooms, and Dogs
A parking lot and accessible, gender-neutral washrooms are available at Glen Lake Beach Park. Dogs are welcome at the off-leash dog beach, and otherwise must be under control and on trails.

Creeks & Watershed
Glen Lake is one of two major lakes in the Colwood Creek Watershed. It is known as an ice kettle lake, as it was formed from a chunk of ice left behind from a melting glacier. Water from the Humpback Reservoir arrives at Glen Lake via Parkdale Creek. Colwood Creek then leads from Glen Lake, passes through Colwood Lake, and eventually empties into the Esquimalt Lagoon at the base of Royal Roads University.

Brasenia schreberi, a plant indigenous to Vancouver Island commonly known as water shield, as seen at Glen Lake.

PHOTO BY ADAM UNGSTAD

Local History

Glen Lake was largely unknown to anyone but locals until the opening of the Galloping Goose Railway encouraged landowners to subdivide their properties for summer cottages. The railroad has since been transformed into the much-loved Galloping Goose Regional Trail, part of a network that stretches from the Swartz Bay ferry terminal to Sooke.

Smoke on the water

On crisp fall mornings, watch for smoke on the water, or steam fog as it is known technically, drifting above a lake's surface.

Water cools slower than land and steam fog forms when cold air drifts across relatively warm water. The air directly above the lake's surface absorbs the heat of the water, rises, mixes with cooler air passing above, and causes water vapour to condense into steam fog.

PHOTO BY ADAM UNGSTAD

Florence Lake

Watershed: Millstream Creek   **Perimeter:** 1.5 km

Elevation: 81 m   **Max Depth:** 5.5 m

Surface: 8.4 ha   **Access:** Florence Lake Road or Springboard Place

Well-hidden behind a busy intersection of the Trans-Canada Highway, Florence Lake is virtually unknown to both visitors and locals alike, although many locals will drive by it every day.

Florence Lake is a great place for an easy stroll with calming views year-round. Around the lake you'll find a boardwalk above wetlands, an accessible viewing deck, and a sunny swimming dock perfect for getting in the water or launching a stand-up paddleboard. Skirt Mountain can be seen to the northwest, and expect a colourful display of leaves in the fall.

Beaches & Swimming
There is no sand beach at Florence Lake, but the pier off Florence Lake Road stretches out into the middle of the lake, providing easy access for swimming in the warm water.

Hikes & Walks
The Strachan Trail, with a distance of about 3 km return, provides a pleasant and flat walk around the south and east sides of the lake. While much of the trail follows Florence Lake Road, there is a raised boardwalk with seating that connects Savory Road with Springboard Place on the south side. This is a wonderful place to sit and enjoy the lake, as well as the marshlands below. Keep your eyes and ears out for songbirds and small critters such as otters and frogs in the undergrowth below.

On the north end of the lake is the Florence Lake Viewing Deck, at the end of an accessible 60 m boardwalk. Looking south, this is perhaps the best view of the lake and the birds and flora that call it home.

Fishing

Florence Lake has not been stocked since 2009. It is a shallow lake, and as such its water warms quickly, making it difficult to support trout. Much of the shoreline is marshy, so take a boat if you do go out.

Paddling & Boats

Parking may be a challenge for those looking to launch a carry-in boat, but there is easy access to do so from the swimming pier at Florence Lake Road. Paddling is a great way to enjoy Florence Lake and explore the riparian ecosystem that lines its shores.

Cycling

To get to Florence Lake by bike, take the Galloping Goose Regional Trail to Thetis Lake Regional Park, then the Thetis-Langford Connector Trail (also known as the Phelps Connector), to get to Treanor Ave. Follow Treanor Ave until it turns into Setchfield Ave and continue until you arrive at Florence Lake Road. Watch for Lake Ida Anne on Treanor Ave.

Accessibility

Most of the Strachan Trail is wide and flat with gradual slopes, with the exception of a steep hill from Savory Road to the boardwalk on the south side. The viewing platform at the north end is wheelchair accessible and has close parking. There are no accessible washrooms at Florence Lake.

Parking, Washrooms, and Dogs

Parking is available at the Florence Lake Viewing Dock and a few other parking spots can also be found along Florence Lake Road. There are no toilets provided at Florence Lake. Dogs must be under control and on trails.

Creeks & Watershed

Florence Lake is part of the Millstream Creek watershed. Water enters Florence Lake via a seasonal tributary off Skirt Mountain known locally as Sometime Creek. The outflow is in the wetlands at southeast corner of the lake, where an unnamed creek carries water eastwards towards a culvert underneath the highway before joining Millstream Creek and ultimately emptying into the Esquimalt Harbour.

Local History

There is some debate about how Florence Lake was named. While the registry of BC Geographic Names states that the lake was named after Florence Isabella Langford, Captain Edward Langford's fifth daughter, other local historians believe it was named after early settlers Henry and Florence Dumbleton, who once owned property at Pike Lake.

Did you know?

Unconfirmed local lore tells the story of a piano at the bottom of Florence Lake. Homes were built on the west side of the lake before there were roads to them, meaning the only way to transport things there was by boat. Apparently one owner tried to bring a piano to their home and lost it in the lake when the boat capsized. If this is a true story, it's likely the piano is still there.

Why do fish jump?

If you've ever been to a salmon run at Goldstream Provincial Park you'll have seen salmon leap out of running water to clear obstacles on their way to spawning grounds upstream. Yet trout will also jump out of a lake's surface on a late summer's afternoon, when they are not spawning and there are no obstacles to clear.

So why do fish jump a lake's surface? The most likely reason is that they are escaping a predator, such as a larger fish chasing them from below. Some fish jump to catch insects, others when they are startled by noise, and it's entirely possible that some might even do it just for fun.

Why do fish move in schools?

Some fish, such as smallmouth bass, move together in a coordinated fashion, a phenomenon known as 'schooling'. When fish swim independently but still remain part of a social group it is called 'shoaling'. Why do fish stick together like this?

The most basic answer is simply, survival. A group of fish can confuse and disorient predators, and having more eyes together makes it easier to watch for predators in the first place, or to find food. Being close to each other also makes it easier to find a mate.

Fish aren't the only species that move together in groups. Canada geese fly in formations to reduce drag in the air (a technique borrowed by racing cyclists), and wolves travel in packs to look after their young while defending their common territory.

Why are fish scales slimy?

From the red stripe across the body of a rainbow trout, to the flamboyant, inverted colours of Dolly Varden, fish scales are a marvel if you stop to look at them. Some fish scales have growth rings, just like the rings found in a cross section of a tree trunk – these growth rings have been used since the late 1800s to determine the age of fish. Unlike trees, fish scales will often show numerous growth rings for each year.

Fish scales are slimy for a reason. They are covered in a coating of mucus to protect the fish from fungus and parasites. When you catch and release fish, wet your hands first to help them keep their slime coat intact.

Lake Ida Anne.
PHOTO BY ADAM UNGSTAD

Lake Ida Anne

This small urban lake found on Treanor Avenue and Ashley Place is used mostly as a place to teach kids about fishing – both technique and ethics. To learn more or register for a program, contact the Freshwater Fisheries Society of BC. The lake is regularly stocked with catchable rainbow trout.

A partially forested walking path circles the lake, showcasing a mix of alder, arbutus, willow, cedar, and spruce. Bring a picnic lunch with you, as there are tables and seating. Midway through the trail on the northern side you'll find another short trail that leads up to the end of Jaimie Place, while an additional trail from the end of Ashley Place leads to Millstream Road. Parking is along Treanor Avenue and launching carry-in boats is permitted on the lake.

Lake Ida Anne is a humanmade feature and acts as a catchment for storm runoff from Bear Mountain. Water leaves the lake via Gardner Creek on the eastern side and makes its way in the Esquimalt Harbour via Millstream Creek. There is a fountain and a small island in the lake.

Colwood

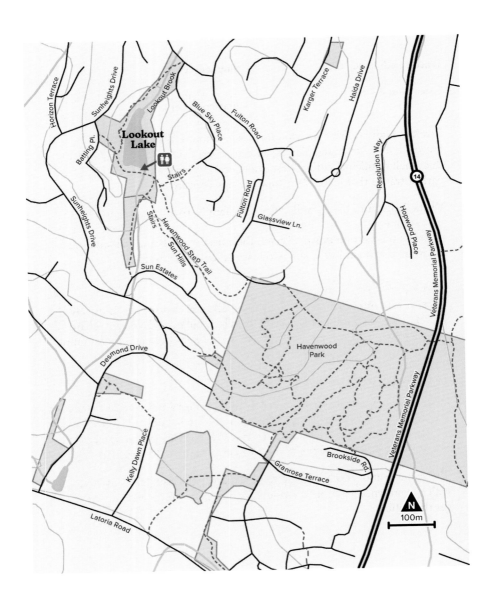

Lookout Lake

Watershed: Bilston Creek

Surface: 0.5 ha

Elevation: 157 m

Access: Lookout Lake Park
(Batting Place)

Perched high on Triangle Mountain is Lookout Lake Park, a local favourite for swimming, picnics, and shoreline fishing. The popularity of this small municipal park is best evidenced by a sign at the Batting Place park entrance that reads "No Rope Swings Permitted."

While Lookout Lake is well-known for family-friendly shoreline fishing, humans aren't the only ones that enjoy the trout in the lake: watch for eagles as they swoop down to catch their next meal. Bring the kids and enjoy an afternoon in the sun with easy access to the water.

Beaches & Swimming
There is no sand beach at Lookout Lake, and the main access is mostly gravel. Entry to the water is easy but can be a bit steep. Expect to share the shoreline with anglers. There is a picnic table at the main access point, and a bench on a small trail that branches off the main trail.

Hikes & Walks
A short distance from the main access to the water are two sets of stairs. The first leads downwards to the Havenwood Steps Trail, which will take you to a small forested urban hike in Havenwood Park below. Expect to find more well-groomed trails when you arrive at this 40-acre park.

The second set of stairs leads up to the summit of Triangle Mountain, which is crowned with private homes and doesn't offer much of a view for the public.

Fishing

The lake is stocked heavily for a lake of its size, generally with rainbow trout. It is best suited for shoreline casting (small spoons and spinners) or still fishing with a bobber and worm. Using artificial eggs near the bottom of the lake is a good strategy for the trout. Smallmouth bass may be present as well.

Paddling & Boats

Lookout Lake is suitable for carry-in boats but it may not be worth the effort given its small size. Stand-up paddleboarders may enjoy a quick paddle, but likely the best boating option at Lookout Lake is something small and inflatable for the kids.

Cycling

There is no direct trail access to Lookout Lake, but you can get most of the way there along the Galloping Goose Regional Trail, from which point onwards you'll need to share roads with cars. Be prepared for some inclines as you approach the lake, as it is situated near the summit of Triangle Mountain.

Accessibility

The short and level trail from Batting Place is too steep to be considered wheelchair accessible, but can be done with a stroller. There are no accessible parking stalls.

Parking, Washrooms, and Dogs

There is no designated parking at Lookout Lake Park, however there is space for a few cars to park on the side of Batting Place. Seasonal toilets are provided, and dogs must be on a leash while in the park.

Creeks & Watershed

Lookout Lake is part of the Bilston Creek watershed. Water leaves the lake via the Lookout Brook and passes through Pritchard Creek and Bilston Creek before emptying into Witty's Lagoon. The original Lookout Brook Dam was built in 1958 and then upgraded in 2020.

Colwood Lake

Colwood Lake is tucked between the Royal Colwood Golf Club and Aldeane Road, which runs parallel to the Galloping Goose Regional Trail. There is access to the lake from Aldeane Road.

This small urban lake is primarily of interest to anglers. There are no trails or infrastructure, but the lake is regularly stocked with rainbow trout. The lake has a maximum depth of 5 meters, with the deep end being farthest from the access point. The easy access from the road makes it possible to launch a canoe or a float-tube. The best fishing for trout is in the spring and fall.

Colwood Lake is part of the Colwood Creek watershed. Much of the water in Colwood Lake originates in the Humpback Reservoir and passes through Irwin Ponds and Glen Lake before reaching Colwood Lake. Colwood Creek then moves onwards, eventually passing through the grounds of the Royal Roads University and emptying into the Esquimalt Lagoon below. A trail on the university grounds, Charlie's Trail, follows Colwood Creek on its final descent to the ocean.

The smell of rain

The word "petrichor" is used to describe the pleasant smell that accompanies the first rain after a long period of warm, dry weather.

On Vancouver Island you can watch the entire cycle of water. Precipitation falls from clouds into watersheds, often moving through lakes via streams and rivers before emptying into the Pacific Ocean. Water in the ocean then evaporates into tiny droplets and becomes clouds again.

While you're at the lake, be sure to look up and marvel at the water floating above you in the sky. Just like your email account, you could say that lakes use "cloud storage". You might notice, too, that lakes change their colour based on what's in the sky at the time.

There are three basic types of clouds: cirrus clouds are thin and wispy, cumulus clouds are big and puffy, and stratus clouds are grey, low-lying sheets.

After a moment or two admiring the lake and its surroundings, look up again. Even just few minutes later, the sky will almost certainly have changed, with clouds rearranging themselves according to wind and pressure, ensuring life on earth by moving the water cycle along.

Malahat

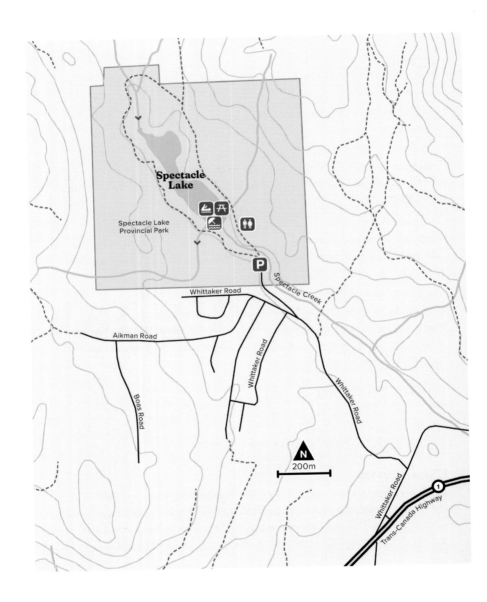

Spectacle Lake

Watershed: Saanich Inlet

Perimeter: 1.2 km

Elevation: 379 m

Max Depth: 7 m

Surface: 3.5 ha

Access: Spectacle Lake Provincial Park (Whittaker Road)

Spectacle Lake Provincial Park is cooperatively managed by the Province of BC and the Cowichan Valley Regional District. Bring your binoculars and camera when you visit, as this is a scenic place with a trail that leads through numerous ecosystems to explore.

There are plenty of birds to watch and listen to in the surrounding forests. The park features a sand beach with picnic tables, and other viewpoints and benches found along the loop trail.

Historical records show that Spectacle Lake was used for skating as the lake would freeze over regularly in years past, however this does not happen often now – possibly a sign of climate change. The lake has also been home to a rare species of fish, eastern brook trout, however there have been few reports of these fish here in recent years.

Beaches & Swimming

The sunny sand beach has an easy, shallow transition into the water, making it perfect for small kids. There are other access points on the east side, but some of these will be too steep for kids.

Hikes & Walks

A 2 km hiking trail circles the lake, leading through mature forest and wetlands and crossing over a couple of wooden boardwalks on the north side. The path on the east side of the lake is wide, open, and well-groomed, whereas the west side is a rooty single-track through denser trees.

Along the lakeside trail.
PHOTO BY ADAM UNGSTAD

Informal trails branch off the north end towards Oliphant Lake and the Malahat Ridge, but be aware that these trails are on private land. Do not trespass; be sure you have permission to use trails outside of the park before you set foot on them.

Fishing

Spectacle Lake is one of the few lakes on Vancouver Island known to host (or have hosted) eastern brook trout. The lake is stocked regularly with rainbow trout, and smallmouth bass are also present. Casting, trolling, spinning, and still fishing with powerbait or worms will work for trout. Spectacle Lake is also a favourite for dry fly fishing between April and June, given the insects that hatch during that time.

Paddling & Boats

Canoes, kayaks, and stand-up paddleboards are welcome at Spectacle Lake, so bring something to explore the lake's surface while admiring the lilies that border the shoreline. There are no access points to the water on the far (north) side of the lake, so that area should be an interesting paddle.

Cycling

Given its access off the Malahat, it is difficult to arrive at Spectacle Lake by bike. An option for experienced long-distance cyclists is to take the Sooke Hills Wilderness Trail and then use Goldstream Heights Drive and Shawnigan Lake Road. You'll still need to ride along the Malahat for about 700 m before reaching Whittaker Road. Note that the Sooke Hills Wilderness Trail is very challenging – there are few options for water, many steep changes in grade, and few options to exit the trail system if needed.

Accessibility

The trail from the parking lot to the beach is wide, well-groomed, and relatively flat. It may not be fully wheelchair accessible, however strollers will be fine. The trail on the eastern side of the lake is wide and has some undulations, likewise not fully accessible for wheelchairs. The trail on the west side of the lake requires sure footing and is not recommended for strollers or people with reduced mobility.

Parking, Washrooms, and Dogs

There is plenty of parking at the lot off Whittaker Road, and pit toilets are available on the trail to the beach. Dogs must be on a leash at all times in the park and are not allowed at the beach.

Local History

You may not be able to see past the trees in the park, but listen closely and you'll notice a difference in the way sound echoes when you are there. The area immediately surrounding the lake is largely clear cut, having originally been logged prior to the 1960s (before the park was established in 1963). It is likely that the area surrounding the park will be developed as residences in the years to come.

Spectacle Lake itself has a rich history of logging and was the site of a sawmill in the early 1900s, which was located on the rocky outcrop close to the main beach. Still to this day, a layer of sawdust lies underneath the main beach and parts of the lake bottom.

Did you know?

Spectacle Lake was named after its shape, which resembles a pair of eyeglasses. Its neighbours, Heart Lake and Stocking Lake, found close to Ladysmith, also take their names from the shape of their perimeters.

Cool stuff about lakes and ice

You won't often see Victoria's lakes frozen over, but here are some "cool" things to know about lakes and ice for when you do come across a frozen lake.

To start with, lake ice melts from the bottom up, not from the top down. Once snow melts, ice on a lake acts like a greenhouse and heats the water underneath. The ice then melts mostly from the bottom, where it is touching the water, as the water is warmer than the air above.

Water from a lake freezes at a different temperature than water from the ocean. While freshwater freezes at 0 ° Celsius, saltwater freezes at about -2 ° Celsius due to its salt content.

If you've ever been lucky enough to walk across a frozen lake, you may have seen bubbles frozen beneath the surface. These are mesmerizing to look at and give perspective to just how thick the ice is below you. Often these bubbles are created by methane, a gas produced by bacteria feeding on the decaying organic matter far below.

Never walk on the surface of a frozen lake unless it is clearly marked as being safe to do so.

PHOTO BY ADAM UNGSTAD

Wrigglesworth Lake

Watershed: Arbutus Creek

Elevation: 352 m

Surface: 2.8 ha

Perimeter: 0.7 km

Max Depth: 14.5 m

Access: Wrigglesworth Community Park (Goldstream Heights Drive)

Wrigglesworth Lake is a well-deserved reward for hikers and cyclists finishing the challenging 13 km Sooke Hills Wilderness Trail. There are no developed facilities or sand beach, but a clearing makes it easy to get into the water for those looking to swim or paddle. At the time of writing, Wrigglesworth Lake had not been stocked by the Freshwater Fisheries Society of BC.

The lake is found in Wrigglesworth Community Park, which was recently created as a by-product of the Goldstream Heights subdivision. Goldstream Heights Drive borders the park on its east side, and the Sooke Hills Wilderness Trail passes through the park on the west side of the lake, but surprisingly there is no direct access between the trail and the lake. Going from the Sooke Hills Wilderness Trail and Wrigglesworth Lake requires a small detour via Trail Way and Goldstream Heights Drive.

Similar to Spectacle Lake (found in a provincial park farther up the Malahat), the trees that border the shorelines of Wrigglesworth Lake can be deceiving, as most of the area in the vicinity has been logged and will likely see significant development in the years to come.

Wrigglesworth Lake is the main body of water in the Arbutus Creek Watershed. Wrigglesworth Brook is the primary inflow to the lake on the west side, and the primary outflow is Arbutus Creek on the south side. This takes water from the lake on an epic journey, flowing beneath the Malahat via a culvert and eventually emptying into Finlayson Arm 350 m below.

Local History

Wrigglesworth Lake takes its name from Joseph Wrigglesworth, who owned property around the lake. A 1910 edition of the Victoria Daily Colonist describes a unique skill Mr. Wrigglesworth had: discovering water underground using only a stick, otherwise known as water divining.

MR. JOSEPH WRIGGLESWORTH, WATER DIVINER.

Image originally printed in the 5 June 1910 edition of the Victoria Colonist, and reprinted with permission from the Times Colonist.

Under the headline "Vancouver Island's Noted Water Witch" the article describes his abilities:

"With a slender, pliable fragment of a tree cut into the shape of a chicken's breast bone, he possesses the miraculous gift of being able to discover springs and basins of water which may have their origin over a hundred feet below the surface of the ground."

The article includes a photograph of Mr. Wrigglesworth blindfolded while at work discovering water beneath the ground he is standing on and credits him with discovering over 150 wells on southern Vancouver Island, further stating that "in no single instance has he met with failure."

Metchosin

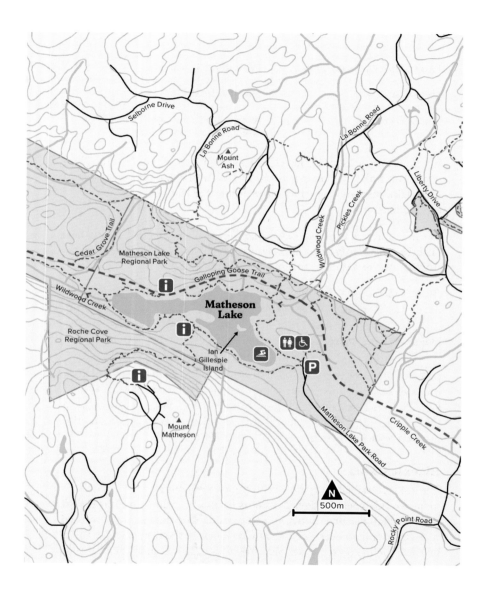

Matheson Lake

Watershed: Wildwood Creek

Perimeter: 3.4 km

Elevation: 21 m

Max Depth: 5 m

Surface: 22.0 ha

Access: Matheson Lake Regional Park
(Matheson Lake Park Road)

Referred to as a "precious jewel" in a 1979 edition of the Victoria Times, Matheson Lake is a wonderful place found at the base of a steep coastal mountain, surrounded by mid-growth forest with plenty of trails to explore nearby.

With easy access from the Galloping Goose Regional Trail, a sand beach, facilities, and plenty of fishing opportunities, it will take many visits to truly know the nature of this magical place.

Bring a blanket for the beach or find a pleasant viewpoint along the northern side of the lakeside trail.

Beaches & Swimming

A great place to swim. Aside from the family-friendly beach near the parking lot, experienced swimmers will enjoy Ian Gillespie Island, which offers space to lie down and soak up the sun after a good swim. While you are there be sure to say a friendly hello to the colony of peaceful ants that call the little island home. Watch for other access points along the northern side of the lake.

Hikes & Walks

The 3.4 km trail circling the lake is a good workout and takes longer than many would expect: budget 2-3 hours to do the entire loop. You will pass through Douglas fir, arbutus, and western red cedar trees, cross exposed rock faces, and go over Wildwood Creek before the trail narrows and takes an incline on the south side. You'll want better shoes than flip-flops!

Swimmers on Ian Gillespie Island at Matheson Lake.
PHOTO BY ADAM UNGSTAD

There are many scenic views of the lake along the loop trail. Watch for yellow skunk cabbage at the far (west) end, and birds such as chickadees, woodpeckers, and Steller's jays along your way.

An easier loop is to take the north side of the lake trail and return to the main parking via the Galloping Goose. The Cedar Grove Trail, on the other side of the Goose, is also worth exploring.

Fishing
The lake is regularly stocked with rainbow trout. Coastal cutthroat trout and smallmouth bass are present. Dolly Varden, a type of char, can be found here too. Fishing from shore can be a challenge as there are no piers or docks, so a boat or float tube will be handy.

Paddling & Boats
Bring your boat about 300 meters down a ramp from the car park and launch at the main beach. The western arm of the lake is an interesting, somewhat eerie place to explore. Boats with electric motors are permitted.

Cycling
A fantastic destination for cyclists, Matheson Lake is about 30 km from Victoria and has a direct connection with the Galloping Goose Regional Trail. Bikes are not allowed in the park, but ample bike racks are provided at the parking lot.

Accessibility
The short trail to the main beach (approx. 100 m) is wheelchair accessible. The loop around the lake requires sure footing and is not recommended for strollers or wheelchairs.

The nearby Galloping Goose Regional Trail offers an accessible alternative, with a few glimpses of the lake and an option to end at the parking lot in Roche Cove Regional Park, about 4 km to the west.

Parking, Washrooms, and Dogs
Parking is at the end of Matheson Lake Park Road. Accessible toilets are available close to the main beach. Dogs are not permitted on the main beach between June 1 and September 15 except to pass through on a leash without stopping.

Creeks & Watershed
Matheson Lake is the only lake in the Wildwood Creek watershed. Water originating in Pickles Creek to the northwest of the lake joins Wildwood Creek, then flows into Matheson Lake. The primary outflow is at the far west corner of the lake, where Wildwood Creek takes water to Roche Cove. Cripple Creek is close by to the southeast of the lake but is part of a different watershed.

Did you know?
Indigenous lore tells of all-powerful giants called sheyeyas who guard Matheson Lake. Superior in intelligence and larger than sasquatches, sheyeyas are invisible and can take on any shape they wish. It is believed that the sheyeyas took the shapes of swans to guard Matheson Lake in years past.

Matheson Lake in Metchosin, BC.
PHOTO BY MIKE MUNROE

Local History

At some point you may wonder about the unique shape of Matheson Lake. A large arm stretches out west and has a very different feel than the rest of the lake, with steep slopes along its shoreline.

Looking at a map of the larger area provides some clues: Roche Cove to the northwest stretches towards this arm of Matheson Lake from the Sooke Basin, and to the southeast Pedder Bay also makes a big reach towards Matheson Lake. Indeed, in the 1860s Matheson Lake was modified in an attempt to create a deep water canal between Pedder Bay, Matheson Lake, and Roche Cove, which would have made East Sooke an island.

Matheson Lake Regional Park was created from donated land from the Matheson family in the 1950s. The lake was previously referred to as Big Lake in an early Victoria directory, and has also been known as Ash Lake after Dr. John Ash, who once owned the land and attempted to create the canal between Roche Cove and Pedder Bay.

Pacific banana slugs

Believe it or not, but those slow-moving, slimy slugs you see slithering around after the rain probably have more interesting lives than you do.

To start with, slugs have both male and female reproductive organs, meaning that when slugs mate, both partners can conceive and lay eggs. Slugs are most active at night, and are known to have up to 27,000 denticles (teeth) – a handy feature, as many slugs on Vancouver Island are known to be cannibals!

The mucus left by slugs helps them to move by smoothing their path across the ground, and also serves as a navigation system, providing a map back to their tunnels and feeding sites.

The much-loved Pacific banana slug is indigenous to Vancouver Island. It is large compared to most slugs, and eats living or decaying vegetation, algae, animal droppings, and even carcasses. Mushrooms are its favourite food.

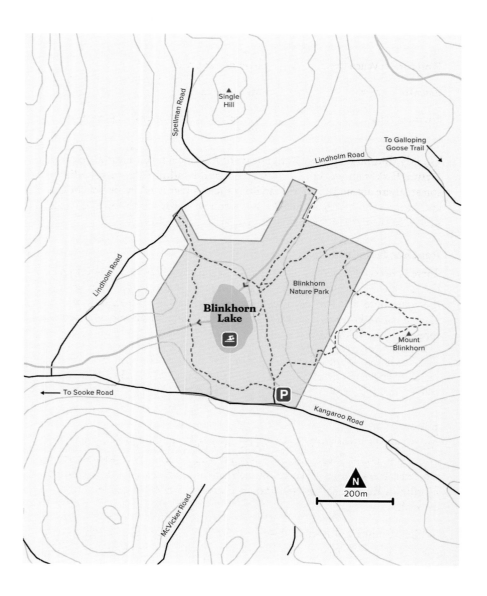

Blinkhorn Lake

Watershed: Veitch Creek

Perimeter: 0.4 km

Elevation: 123 m

Max Depth: 6 m

Surface: 1.1 ha

Access: Blinkhorn Nature Park (Kangaroo Road)

Quietly shimmering away in the heart of Metchosin, Blinkhorn Lake Nature Park is an ideal place for a quiet stroll to admire the surrounding forest. There are no developed facilities such as picnic tables or benches, and likewise no beach at the lake, but a couple of rooty and forested access points provide pleasant places for a pause and reflection.

Beaches & Swimming

There is no sand beach at Blinkhorn Lake and the main access point on the south side is shaded and rooty, so it's best to count on being in or on the water here. The natural shoreline makes Blinkhorn Lake a unique place to swim however, as all you see from the water is the surrounding forest and the skies above.

A fallen log at the north east corner of the lake provides a more secluded space to get in. You may even get lucky and have this corner of lake all to yourself.

Hikes & Walks

An enjoyable, mostly level trail circles the lake, which takes about 30 minutes to complete and leads through maple, Douglas fir, and western red cedar trees. Two small trails branch off the north end and lead towards Lindholm Road, although the eastern branch is for fire and emergency use only.

While Mount Blinkhorn is close by, there is no public access to its summit, which is beyond park boundaries. On your walk around the lake you may notice a small rise between the trail and the lake on the south side, where evidence remains of a cabin.

The indigenous *Nuphar polysepala*, commonly known as pond lilies, along the shore of Blinkhorn Lake.

PHOTO BY ADAM UNGSTAD

Fishing

Blinkhorn Lake offers good fishing for rainbow trout and is generally stocked with the Blackwater River strain every two years. Most of the shoreline is lined with trees and aquatic vegetation and there is no pier to cast from, so a float tube or carry-in boat will be useful here.

Paddling & Boats

The shoreline at Blinkhorn Lake is largely undisturbed. There are no houses, docks, or beaches, only wetlands, aquatic vegetation, and forests, which makes it a magical place for paddlers to explore. While the main access is close to parking, canoes or kayaks will need to be carried through some trees and over uneven ground to get to the water. Motorized boats are not permitted.

Cycling

Blinkhorn Lake is a great cycling destination. Taking the Galloping Goose Regional Trail, exit at Morland Road and then follow Kangaroo Road for the last 2 km. An alternative, if you'd like a good workout at the finish, is to take the climb on Lindholm Road.

Accessibility

The trail around the lake is generally flat, wide, and easy to navigate, however it is not wheelchair accessible. The eastern side of the lake is the most user-friendly and is appropriate for strollers. The west side has some undulations and occasional rocks to navigate.

Parking, Washrooms, and Dogs

Limited parking is available at Kangaroo Road trailhead, and there is no parking along Lindholm Road. There are no washrooms or toilets provided at Blinkhorn Lake Nature Park. Dogs must be under control and on trails.

Creeks & Watershed

Blinkhorn Lake is part of the Veitch Creek watershed. An unnamed creek on the west side of the lake is the primary outflow, which joins Veitch Creek. Veitch Creek flows southwards and empties into Hutchinson Cove in the Sooke Basin.

Local History

Blinkhorn Lake takes its name from an enterprising and free-spirited couple, Thomas and Anne Blinkhorn. The Blinkhorns set foot on Vancouver Island in 1851, and along with James Cooper are considered the first truly independent settlers of the island – that is, they were the first settlers who were not direct employees of the Hudson's Bay Company. Before arriving with in Vancouver Island, Thomas Blinkhorn spent time in Australia (as a convict), which may have influenced the naming of Kangaroo Road.

The Blinkhorns ran the Bilston Farm in the area now known as Witty's Lagoon, and for many years their farm was the only settlement between Sooke and Fort Victoria. At the time, Indigenous people lived on the beach below the farm, and the Blinkhorns would hire their canoes as transport to Fort Victoria.

Thomas and Anne's daughter Martha kept a diary from 1853 to 1856, which is the only known diary written by a woman on Vancouver Island prior to the gold rush. In 1867 Bilston farm was sold to John Witty, who had left the San Juan Islands for political reasons.

The uniquely shaped Blinkhorn Peninsula near Alert Bay also appears to have been named after this family. There is a recreation site on the peninsula.

Blinkhorn Lake was originally set aside by the Capital Regional District as a potential water supply, but then transferred to the municipality of Metchosin as parkland in 1998.

Glinz Lake

(Restricted access)

Nestled in the Sooke foothills, Glinz Lake is the home of a unique outdoor branch of the YMCA-YWCA of Vancouver Island, called Camp Thunderbird. Many happy memories of the outdoors, music, and campfires are made here.

The lands around Glinz Lake are privately owned, so if you are not participating in a programme offered by Camp Thunderbird, you'll need permission to visit. Swimming, boating, and fishing are not permitted for the public due to health and safety concerns, but hiking is occasionally permitted for organized groups.

Camp Thunderbird offers activities including swimming, canoeing, archery, orienteering, hiking, and team building for youth in grades 1–12. Programs for families and customized outdoor education are also available. Facilities can be rented to host up to 140 people overnight, which includes access to the network of trails leading through the 1200-acre surrounding forest.

A trail with hand-built bridges circles Glinz Lake, featuring interpretive signs about the surrounding forest: a medley of Sitka spruce, red alder, hemlock, grand fir, and Douglas fir provide homes for birds like Lorquin's admirals and Steller's jay. If you are there at just the right time you may even see a great horned owl!

Glinz Lake is part of the Ayum Creek watershed. Ayum Creek feeds into Glinz lake on the north side and leaves on the south side, eventually emptying into Cooper Cove (Sooke Basin) below.

Local History

Brothers Leonard and Arnold Glinz arrived on Vancouver Island from Switzerland in the early 1911, and while exploring the wilderness of the Sooke area found the lake that now carries their family name.

The lake was an ideal place for a hunting cabin, and as there was no road to the lake, they built their own, enabling them to bring hunting supplies several kilometres uphill. The Glinz family kept the hunting cabin as a holiday and hunting retreat until the 1930s, and then decided to make it available as a children's camp, which is how Camp Thunderbird came to be.

Sea to Sea Regional Park

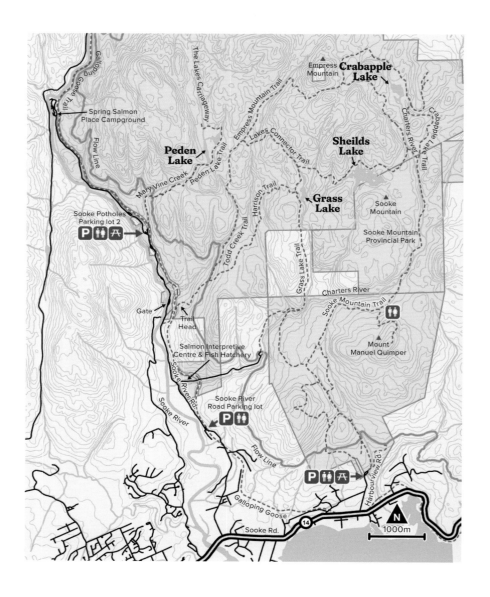

Crabapple Lake

Watershed: Sooke River

Perimeter: 1.8 km

Elevation: 427 m

Max Depth: 10 m

Surface: 5.8 ha

Access: Sea to Sea Regional Park (Harbour-view Road)

Crabapple Lake is a quiet beauty, deep in the heart of the Sea to Sea Regional Park. Expect pink water lilies in the summer and a bit of calm at this small, hike-in lake.

Its relatively remote location and the three-hour uphill hike needed to get there mean that few people venture up to see it, and if they do it's often a quick detour on the way to its larger neighbour, Sheilds Lake, or up to the summit of Mount Empress for panoramic views of the horizon. The surrounding second-growth forest is not as mature as one might expect, but still home to a wide range of animals and plants.

Beaches & Swimming
Crabapple Lake is a pleasant place for a dip and a picnic after the hike to get there, but don't expect a beach! Much of the shoreline is marshy, so be sure not to disturb the resident riparian life if you choose to get in.

Hikes & Walks
Regardless of your starting point, expect a moderate to challenging three-hour hike (each way) to get to the lake. The out-and-back route via Sooke Mountain Trail is easiest to follow, but with some planning and experience there are many hiking options in the area. Watch the treeline for a single Douglas fir tree with a diameter of over 3 meters as you approach via the Crabapple Lake Trail.

In years past it was difficult to access Crabapple Lake via the Sooke Mountain Trail during the wet season, as parts of the trail would be

Nymphaea odorata, an aquatic plant commonly known as water lily, lines the surface near the shore of Crabapple Lake.
PHOTO BY ADAM UNGSTAD

washed out by the Charters River. A new multi-use aluminum bridge was installed as part of the opening of the Lakes Section of the Sea to Sea Regional Park in late 2019, providing easier access for hikers during all seasons.

Late 2020 saw the opening of the southern portion of the Sooke Hills Wilderness Regional Park, with a number of new trails and routes to Crabapple Lake starting from Sooke Road. Crabapple Lake is wilderness territory, and you may encounter black bears, cougars, or wolves. Never hike alone.

Fishing

Crabapple Lake has not been stocked since 2009 but you can still expect to find small rainbow trout. Given the hike in, float tubes or angling from the shore are ideal.

Paddling & Boats

Something light and inflatable will be the best type of vessel for this small, hike-in lake.

Cycling

Cycling all the way up to Crabapple Lake is a long climb, but having a bike saves time and energy on the way down. The Galloping Goose Regional Trail intersects with Harbourview Road, which is the trailhead for the Sooke Mountain Trail.

If you are starting from Victoria, it is possible to put your bike on a bus, get off at Harbourview Road, cycle up to Crabapple Lake, and then return via the Galloping Goose. Start early however as this will be a very long but satisfying trip!

There is network of mountain biking trails at the end of Harbourview Road, where a wash station and bike racks are provided.

Accessibility

Unfortunately, due to the length of the hike required to get there and the sometimes rocky state of the trail, Crabapple Lake is not accessible for strollers or people with limited mobility.

Parking, Washrooms, and Dogs

Designated parking is at the end of Harbourview Road. Pit toilets are available at the parking lot or farther along the Sooke Mountain Trail.

Dogs must be on a leash at all times. This protects dogs and their owners from encounters with black bears, cougars, or wolves, and likewise protects the resident plants and animals from harassment and disturbance.

Creeks & Watershed

Crabapple Lake is the headwaters of the small but mighty Charters River, which eventually feeds into the Sooke River to the west. Restoration and rehabilitation by volunteers and local governments has encouraged salmon spawning at the base of the Charters River, and an interpretive centre hosted by the Juan de Fuca Salmon Restoration Society can be found on Sooke River Road.

Local History

A cabin used to exist at Crabapple Lake, and while it is gone now you may still see some concrete remnants when you visit. The cabin had a stone fireplace and was built by Eric Bernard, who ran a well-known logging and pole-cutting operation in the area, so he could share weekend retreats with his wife, Marjorie, at the lake. Bernard is credited with bringing pink water lilies to Crabapple Lake. It is likely that the lake received its name from this couple, who admired the Pacific crab apples growing along the shore.

What is now known as the Sooke Mountain Trail was actually a paved road in the 1940s and 1950s. It was originally called Mount Shepherd Road, and pieces of the pavement can still be seen in the rockier sections.

Like its neighbour, Sheilds Lake, Crabapple Lake was used for skating by pioneering locals in the winters of the early 1900s.

Pacific crab apple

Crab apple trees don't get much attention on Vancouver Island, as we usually focus on the tall trees such as Douglas firs, or the flashier arbutus and Garry oak. Yet Pacific crab apple trees have their own claim to fame: they are British Columbia's only indigenous apple tree.

These are deciduous trees (sometimes multi-stemmed shrubs) and are found along lakesides and streams throughout Vancouver Island. These trees can grow to be up to 12 metres tall and have white flowers from April to June. At two centimetres across, their fruit is much smaller than the cultivated varieties of crab apple found in suburban backyards – these apples look more like berries.

Pacific crab apples are high in acid, which helps them to keep for long periods of time, providing a source of food in the winter for deer, bears, mice, and birds. Coastal Indigenous people also took advantage of this feature – because of their acidity, the apples could be stored underwater for long periods of time.

The far arm of Sheilds Lake.
PHOTO BY ADAM UNGSTAD

Sheilds Lake

Watershed: Sooke River

Elevation: 425 m

Surface: 14.3 ha

Perimeter: 3.2 km

Max Depth: 16 m

Access: Sea to Sea Regional Park (Sooke River Road or Harbourview Road)

Located south of Empress Mountain, Sheilds Lake has long been a favourite for outdoor enthusiasts and is a stunning place to spend an afternoon. You'll want to leave early for the hike to get there so you can admire the ferns, wildflowers, Manzanita shrubs, arbutus, and Garry oak trees on the way. This lake is a beauty any time of year and was once known as the Lake of the Seven Hills after the mountains and peaks that surround it.

The north side of the lake gets plenty of sun, with a number of access points and an outcrop providing a nice view of the islands in the lake. In the right season, look for salamanders lining the shore just below the surface of the water.

On the southwest corner is a more open area with trace remains of an old lodge owned by the Alpine Club of Canada. At this clearing you may see what appears to be trail along the southern side of the lake, but beware that this trail currently dissolves into dense, largely impassable forest. The change in the trail may be because this lake has its shores in two different parks: Sea to Sea Regional Park and Sooke Mountain Provincial Park.

Because of its altitude, the air at Sheilds Lake can be up to ten degrees cooler than at sea level, and the lake sometimes sparkles with thin ice in January. In the mid-1900s, Sooke residents would make the trek up to the lake to spend the day skating.

Beaches & Swimming

There is no sand beach, but there are a handful of access points where the brave can enjoy a good, brisk swim.

Sheilds Lake.
PHOTO BY ADAM UNGSTAD

Hikes & Walks

There are many routes to get to Sheilds Lake, and part of the fun is doing them all so you can choose your favourite. For lake enthusiasts, the best route is to take the Peden Lake Trail and then the Lakes Connector Trail. On this route you'll be able to visit three lakes (with a small but worthwhile detour to Grass Lake).

The route easiest to follow is via the Sooke Mountain Trail, which starts from the end of Harbourview Road. However, experienced hikers will likely prefer one of the single-track routes leaving from Sooke River Road.

The Grass Lake Trail branches off Sooke River Road near the salmon interpretive centre. Other trailheads include the Todd Creek Trail and the Harrison Trail (which share the same trailhead), or the Peden Lake Trail. Any of these routes will pass by Grass Lake before you reach Sheilds Lake.

For the best view of Sheilds Lake, make your way north to two peaks known as the Dumbbells (named due to their shape). Puzzle Peak, to the north west of Sheilds Lake offers, splendid views of the neighbouring

Grass Lake. The summit of Empress Mountain, the highest peak in the CRD, is accessible via the Todd Creek Trail and offers a spectacular vista of the entire area.

Regardless how you get there, wake up early and get a head start, as time passes quickly at Sheilds Lake. Budget three hours each way. This is wilderness territory, and you may encounter black bears, cougars, or wolves. Never hike alone.

Fishing
Sheilds Lake has not been stocked since 2009 but rainbow and coastal cutthroat trout are present. Given the hike in, float-tubes or angling from the shore are ideal. It's a great place for fly fishing.

Paddling & Boats
Given the hike required, bring something inflatable to float on or take your chances and hope that there is a boat waiting for you there. There are many different islands in the lake to visit.

Cycling
The Galloping Goose Regional Trail connects with all trailheads along Sooke River Rd. Cycling is not permitted on the Harrison Trail or the Peden Lake Trail, however, so use either the Grass Lake Trail or the Todd Creek Trail. Note that the Spring Salmon Place Campground on Sooke RiverRoad has reduced rates for cyclists.

Mountain bikers should also visit the Harbourview Road trailhead, where the CRD has developed trails and infrastructure specifically for mountain biking. Cycling is also permitted along the Sooke Mountain Trail.

Accessibility
The route to Sheilds Lake is recommended only for experienced wilderness hikers. The Galloping Goose Regional Trail along Sooke River Road offers a user-friendly alternative, with views of Todd Creek from a wooden trestle, and further south, the Charters River.

Parking, Washrooms, and Dogs

There are two parking lots, each with pit toilets available on Sooke River Road. The second lot has accessible parking and toilets. Harbourview Road also has parking and pit toilets, and additional toilets are provided along the Sooke Mountain Trail.

Dogs must be on a leash at all times. This protects dogs and their owners from encounters with bears, cougars, or wolves, while also protecting indigenous animals, plants, and other hikers from disturbance and harassment.

Creeks & Watershed

Sheilds Lake is part of the Sooke River Watershed. Water from Sheilds Lake and its neighbour, Grass Lake, meet in an unnamed creek before flowing into the Charters River. It then moves onwards into the Sooke River.

Local History

There is a persistent rumour that Sheilds Lake was intended to be known as Sheila's Lake, but this is not true. Sheilds Lake was named after the family of James Sheilds, who settled on the west side of the Sooke River in the 1800s.

The two-storey lodge built at Sheilds Lake by the Alpine Club of Canada in 1928 was a popular wilderness retreat in the 1930s. The lodge since burned down but remains can still be seen on the west side of the lake.

Smaller cabins were also built at Sheilds Lake by Scouts Canada and the Boys Club of Victoria, but little physical evidence of these structures remains.

Salamanders, newts, lizards...

March is a good time to look along shorelines for new wriggling life such as salamanders. *Plethodon vehiculum*, commonly known as western redback salamander, makes its home in moist places like decaying logs throughout the Pacific northwest. The presence of these amphibians is an indicator of the overall health of an ecosystem, as they breathe through their pollution-sensitive skin.

A type of salamander that spends plenty of time in lakes and ponds is a newt. *Taricha granulosa*, commonly known as roughskin nnewt, is indigenous to North America and produces a toxin called tetrodotoxin, the same chemical produced by pufferfish. No need to run when you see a newt, however. Just leave it alone and you'll be fine.

Salamanders and newts should not be confused with *Podarcis muralis*, an invasive species commonly known as European wall lizard that is often seen in Victoria's backyards. Lizards are reptiles, so they have scaly, drier skin, and generally have longer legs and toes.

Grass Lake.
PHOTO BY ADAM UNGSTAD

Grass Lake

Watershed: Sooke River

Perimeter: 3.3 km

Elevation: 408 m

Max Depth: 7.6 m

Surface: 8.7 ha

Access: Sea to Sea Regional Park (Sooke River Road)

As one might expect, parts of the shoreline around Grass Lake consist of tall grasses emerging from marshy wetlands. If you are visiting in summer, expect to find stunning water lilies of many shades along the edges of the shoreline. The Lakes Connector Trail, which leads to Grass Lake, was previously known as Camp Tent Pole Trail.

Various maps show different shapes for Grass Lake, indicating that changing water levels have altered the lake's perimeter over the years. A bathymetric map published by the Province of BC in 1969 shows a surface area of 10 hectares for Grass Lake, whereas a technical report published by the Province in 2019 lists a surface area of only 3.5 hectares. Walking along the northern side of the lake you will see remnants of previously submerged land that has been reclaimed by terrestrial or emergent flora.

Devastation Hill lies directly south of Grass Lake. To the north and slightly to the east is Puzzle Peak, which offers splendid views. Pleasant Peak lies between Grass Lake and its larger neighbour, Sheilds Lake, which is a short distance away.

Beaches & Swimming

There is no beach at Grass Lake, but the rock outcrop is a perfect place for a refreshing dip after your hike to get there.

Fishing

Grass Lake has not been stocked since 2009, but you can still expect to find small rainbow and cutthroat trout. It's best for spincasting or fly fishing.

Hikes & Walks

There are many ways to get to Grass Lake. The Peden Lake Trail, which connects to the Lakes Connector Trail via a short stretch of the Todd Creek Trail, is a great option and offers an enjoyable stop at Peden Lake on the way.

The Harrison Trail leads past basalt cliffs, impressive sword ferns, and plenty of salal. This trail is rocky and often more difficult than anticipated. Budget at least 6 hours (return) for the journey and be prepared for a good climb. Along the way you'll pass the Sooke Flowline and will likely see an abandoned car from a different era being slowly claimed by the forest.

Paddling & Boats

Given the hike, you'll need to bring an inflatable if you want something to float on. Most human visitors to the lake will stay close to the rock outcrop, but this is one of the more interesting shorelines to explore in the area.

Cycling

The Galloping Goose Regional Trail connects with all trailheads along Sooke River Rd. Cycling is not permitted on the Harrison Trail or the Peden Lake Trail, so use the Grass Lake Trail if you are taking your bike. Note that the Spring Salmon Place Campground on Sooke River Road has reduced rates for cyclists.

Accessibility

The route to Grass Lake is recommended only for experienced wilderness hikers. The Galloping Goose Regional Trail along Sooke River Road offers a user-friendly alternative, with views of Todd Creek from a trestle and the Charters River farther south.

Parking, Washrooms, and Dogs

There are two parking lots, each with pit toilets, available on Sooke River Road. The second parking lot has accessible parking and toilets. Dogs must be on a leash at all times. This protects dogs and their owners from encounters with bears, cougars, or wolves, while also protecting indigenous animals, plants, and other hikers from disturbance and harassment.

Creeks & Watershed

Grass Lake is part of the Sooke River Watershed. Water leaves the lake via an unnamed creek on the south side and feeds into Charters River before connecting with the Sooke River.

Local History

The Harrison Trail takes its name from Claude L. Harrison, who was the 44th mayor of Victoria in the 1950s, the city prosecutor for over 40 years, and an active member of the Alpine Club of Canada. Along Dallas Road in Victoria's James Bay neighbourhood is a small, man-made pond used for model boats, which was also named after Claude L. Harrison.

Ferns

You don't have to go very far on Vancouver Island before coming across a fern. Ferns provide microhabitats and shelter for small animals, and when you find one you'll likely find many growing together. Yet ferns are an unusual plant, as they do not produce flowers or seeds.

At a simplified level, ferns reproduce with microscopic spores. Whereas seeds have multiple layers containing everything a young plant needs to sustain itself, a spore can survive and spread on its own. Reproduction with spores is a form of reproduction without sex. In effect it is a form of cloning: the new tiny plant that develops from the spores contains the same genetic material as its single parent. These tiny plants have reproductive structures, which then undergo sex to produce the larger plant seen growing on the forest floor.

Pay attention to the feather-like, fan-shaped leaves of ferns, and you will begin to notice subtle differences between species like sword fern, deer fern, and braken fern. Sword fern was known by some coastal Indigenous peoples as 'pala-pala plant', as it was used in a child's game: who can pull the most leaflets off in a single breath, while saying 'pala' with each one.

Peden Lake

Watershed: Sooke River

Perimeter: 1.2 km

Elevation: 316 m

Access: Sea to Sea Regional Park (Peden Lake Trail)

Surface: 3.4 ha

Peden Lake has long been a favourite day destination for hikers, swimmers, and naturalists. It is most commonly accessed via the Peden Lake Trail, which leads through an impressive second-growth forest parallel to the Mary Vine Creek and offers a stop at a picturesque waterfall in the wet season.

During your visit watch for eagles high above and Steller's jays, flickers, red squirrels, and black-tailed deer in the surrounding forest. Watch the forest floor for garter snakes, slugs, and insects hard at work.

What is commonly known as Peden Lake is actually two separate bodies of water. The one on the west side is marked as Peden Lake by the Capital Regional District, but the one on the east side is technically unnamed. Some locals call it Upper Peden Lake or refer to the two together as the Peden Lakes. Unofficial maps have also labelled it as Mary Vine Lake.

Beaches & Swimming

The lake has no beach, but there is easy entry to the water at the main access point on the southern lake. Watch for submerged logs.

Fishing

Peden Lake has not been stocked since 2009, but you can still expect to find small rainbow and cutthroat trout. The lake is popular for fly fishing.

Hikes & Walks

The most common route to Peden Lake is via the Peden Lake Trail (3.3 km one way), which starts at Sooke River Road in the Sooke Potholes Regional Park at parking lot #2. The trail leads parallel to Mary Vine Creek among salmonberry bushes, Douglas fir trees, and manzanita

Peden Lake.
PHOTO BY ADAM UNGSTAD

shrubs. It is considered moderate in difficulty, with an elevation gain of 225 m. You will need to use your hands to climb over large rocks in some places.

Cell reception is sparse, so bring a set of offline maps and a friend. Budget two hours each way if you are using the Peden Lake Trail, and longer for other routes.

Paddling & Boats

Bring something light and inflatable to explore the lake by its surface, as you'll need to carry it with you there and back. Alternatively, you may get lucky and find a canoe waiting for you there.

Cycling

All trailheads for routes to Peden Lake along Sooke River Road branch off the Galloping Goose Regional Trail. Cycling is not permitted on the Peden Lake Trail or the Harrison Trail, however, so cyclists must use either the Grass Lake Trail or the Todd Creek Trail to reach Peden Lake.

Accessibility

The route to Peden Lake is recommended only for experienced wilderness hikers. The Galloping Goose Regional Trail along Sooke River Road offers a user-friendly alternative, with views of Todd Creek from a wooden trestle, and farther south, the Charters River.

Parking, Washrooms, and Dogs

Accessible pit toilets are at the trailhead for the Peden Lake Trail in the Sooke Potholes parking lot #2, along Sooke River Road. Dogs must be on a leash at all times. This protects dogs and their owners from encounters with bears, cougars, or wolves, as well as the forest residents from disturbance.

Creeks & Watershed

While Peden Lake is part of the Sooke River Watershed, it does not flow into the Charters River as do Grass Lake, Sheilds Lake, and Crabapple Lake. Water leaves Peden Lake via Mary Vine Creek, which feeds directly into the Sooke River.

Local History

Peden Lake was named after the Peden family, who owned a feed store on Wharf Street in Victoria for many years in the early 1900s and had two sons that grew up to be famous athletes.

William "Torchy" Peden was born in Victoria in 1906 and acquired his nickname after his flaming red hair and ability to lead the pack of long-distance cyclists. During the great depression, he was given a gold-plated bicycle by the Canadian Cycle and Motor Company, which he rode during special exhibitions. His brother, Douglas Peden, competed in the 1936 Olympics and helped bring back a silver medal in basketball for Canada.

Did you know?

For many years, there used to be a one-room research cabin at Peden Lake. This cabin was taken down in 2019 when the Lakes Section of the Sea to Sea Regional Park was officially opened.

Swimming snakes!

The most abundant snake in Canada is the common garter snake (*Thamnophis sirtalis*). There's a good chance you may see one of these swimming in or near a lake on Vancouver Island.

These snakes are non-venomous, meaning their bite is not poisonous. Unlike many other reptiles, these snakes are live bearing, meaning the young live inside their mother until they are born, rather than hatching from eggs. There are usually 10–15 snakelets (baby snakes) per litter.

Common garter snakes are mostly terrestrial and typically hunt during the day, enjoying a good meal of slugs or worms. If you see one swimming in a lake there's a good chance they are hunting for juvenile amphibians such as frogs or salamanders, or small fish.

Snakes are important both as predators and prey. As predators they keep other species populations in balance. As prey they provide food for raptors such as owls and hawks, and other larger predators.

Sooke & Otter Point

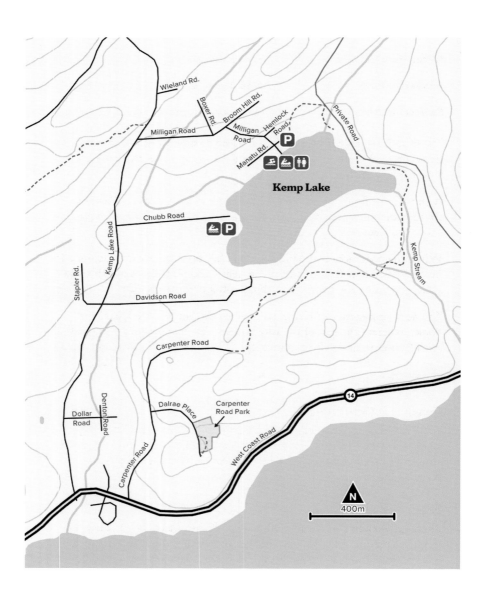

Kemp Lake

Watershed: Kemp Stream

Perimeter: 2.5 km

Elevation: 33 m

Max Depth: 11 m

Surface: 25.0 ha

Access: via Milligan Rd. or Chubb Rd.

The first thing people notice when arriving at Kemp Lake is the pristine, fresh ocean air in the Sooke area. The air at Kemp Lake alone will make your trip worthwhile!

A short drive from Sooke, Kemp Lake is ideal for canoes and kayaks. Bring your fishing rod and a picnic lunch. Watch for wildlife, dragonflies, and water lilies while you are there.

While the boat launch at Milligan Road has been largely undeveloped for many years, a new fishing pier, picnic table, and pit toilet were added in 2020, providing the public with more options to use the lake.

The northeast corner of Kemp Lake generally borders the District of Sooke, whereas the rest of the lake borders the Juan de Fuca Electoral Area (more precisely, the community of Otter Point). Poirier Lake and Broom Hill are to the northeast. There are no parks at Kemp Lake, and most of the shoreline is taken up by private homes.

Beaches & Swimming

As there are no sand beaches, the best option for swimmers at Kemp Lake is to take a boat or an air mattress out into the lake from Milligan Road. The lake bottom at Chubb Road is marshy and generally not pleasant for swimmers.

Hikes & Walks

There are no parks or public trails around Kemp Lake. While there might be private trails on some of the land around the lake, be sure you have permission to be on them and do not trespass. All the shoreline borders private land, except for the access points at Chubb Road and Milligan Road.

The dock on Kemp Lake at Milligan Road.
PHOTO BY FRESHWATER FISHERIES SOCIETY OF BC

Fishing

Stocked regularly with catchable rainbow trout. Coastal cutthroat trout are present as well, and there are rumours of steelhead trout in this lake. Bring a canoe, kayak or float tube to cast from, as the vast majority of the shoreline borders private land. There is a fair amount of aquatic vegetation close to the shore.

Paddling & Boats

Particularly well suited for non-motorized boats or stand-up paddle boards. Carry-in boats can be launched from the west side of the lake at Chubb Road, while Milligan Road offers a launch for larger boats. Motorized boats are not permitted on Kemp Lake.

Strollers & Wheelchairs
Aside from the residences around it, this lake is largely undeveloped for public use. Both access points offer a view of the lake just a short, level stroll from parking. Note that the seasonal toilet at Milligan Road requires navigating 2-3 stairs made of large stones. Getting into the water will be easiest from Milligan Road.

Parking, Washrooms and Dogs
Limited parking at both Chubb Road and Manatu Road. Seasonal toilets available at the Milligan Road boat launch. Dogs must be under control and kept on trails.

Creeks & Watershed
Kemp Lake is a water source for residents of the Otter Point area. There are two inflows to Kemp Lake, the first found at the northern tip and the second on the western side. The primary outflow, Kemp Stream, leaves from the "arm" of the lake on the east side and empties into the Juan de Fuca Strait.

Local History
Kemp Lake was originally known as "Clyde Lake". The current name comes from Richard Kemp, a pioneering settler of the west side of the lake. An early map believed to be from 1894 identifies "Kemp Town", a small settlement of ten buildings located on the lakeshore immediately north of what is now known as Chubb Road.

Poirier Lake

Home of dragonflies, frogs, salamanders, songbirds, and 33 different types of fruit trees, Poirier Lake is a small, scenic lake just a short drive from Sooke. It is an ideal place to spend an afternoon with the extended family.

Most of the shoreline falls in William Simmons Memorial Community Park, which features an all-season group picnic shelter, car-top boat launch, fishing dock, equestrian facilities, and connections to a network of community trails. The area was once a residence, and there is a wide variety of indigenous and introduced plants in the park.

The multi-use gravel trails at Poirier Lake are wide, well-groomed, and level. The boating dock, a short distance from the main parking lot, offers stunning views of water lilies in the summer.

Due to a soft lake bottom and dangerous submerged log debris, swimming is not permitted at Poirier Lake. The fishing dock, not to be confused with the boating dock, is near the deep (west) end of the lake and found via a trail branching off the main Panama Rail Trail. Poirier Lake has been stocked regularly with catchable rainbow trout since 2015.

Aside from the water lilies that grow along the shoreline, the day use area is the star attraction of Poirier Lake. There are few other lakes in the vicinity with group picnic facilities mere steps away from a lake. The fishing dock offers a quieter, more secluded counterpoint. Dogs must be kept on a leash.

While the main parking is just off Otter Point Road, there are two trails that depart from a second parking area off Butler Road. The Weiland Trail (sometimes referred to incorrectly as the Wetland Trail) leads south for about 400 m before heading west towards Kemp Lake Road. On the north side of Otter Point Road is the 1.25 km Butler Trail, which offers a short loop through the Woods subdivision.

There are aspirations to connect the Weiland trail to Kemp Lake, and ultimately to create an extension of the Galloping Goose Regional Trail in the Otter Point Community.

A portion of the parkland at Poirier Lake was donated by Erik Sellars-St. Clare, who lived at the property from 1948 to 2007. Mr. Sellars-St. Clare

The fishing dock at Poirier Lake.
PHOTO BY FRESHWATER FISHERIES SOCIETY OF BC

passed his property to the Capital Regional District through his estate and requested that the park be named after his long-time friend, William Simmons, rather than himself.

Poirier Lake and Kemp Lake are not connected by a stream despite the proximity between the two. Whereas Poirier Lake lies in the DeMamiel Creek Watershed, which empties into the Sooke River, Kemp Lake is part of the Kemp Stream Watershed, which flows directly into the Juan de Fuca Strait.

Poirier Lake is named after the pioneering Poirier family, as is École Poirer in Sooke. Joseph Poirier Sr. was born in Quebec in 1829 and settled with his wife Ellen Brule along the Sooke River around 1850. Poirier worked at a sawmill on Veitch Creek before taking on work as a lumberjack, providing logs for the Muir family business. Joseph Poirier Sr. and Ellen Brule had 12 children together.

Before acquiring its current name in 1934, Poirer Lake was known locally as Hiscocks Lake.

Young Lake
(Restricted access)

Found in the Otter Point community just west of Sooke, Young Lake is the home of Camp Barnard, a 250-acre camp backing onto Mount Bluff and the Sooke Hills. It has been used by Scouts Canada for over 70 years.

Camp Barnard is privately owned and there is no public access to the lake, but non-scouting groups are welcome to rent facilities such as rustic cabins and backcountry or lakeside campsites for their programs. Catering is not provided, which means rental rates are low. Facilities are ideal for events such as team building, training, music retreats, book clubs, art clubs, reunions, and more.

Young Lake is big enough for a good paddle and small enough for great lakeside hiking adventures for children. In the past, jamborees have hosted scouts from around the world.

The camp is named after Senator George Henry Barnard, who donated 200 acres of the land around Young Lake to Scouts Canada in 1945. Barnard served as mayor of Victoria from 1904 to 1905, as a Member of Parliament for Victoria from 1908 to 1917, and as a Canadian senator from 1917 to 1945.

Young Lake is in the DeMamiel Creek watershed. DeMamiel Creek feeds into Young Lake and then carries water onwards to the Sooke River.

Index

Matheson Lake at dusk.
PHOTO BY MURRAY SHARRATT